Perfect
Freelancing

THE PERFECT SERIES

ALL YOU NEED TO GET IT RIGHT FIRST TIME

OTHER TITLES IN THE SERIES:

The Perfect Appraisal by Howard Hudson

Perfect Business Writing by Peter Bartram

The Perfect Business Plan by Ron Johnson

The Perfect Career by Max Eggert

Perfect Communications by Andrew Leigh and Michael Maynard

The Perfect Conference by Iain Maitland

Perfect Customer Care by Ted Johns

The Perfect CV by Max Eggert

Perfect Decisions by Andrew Leigh

The Perfect Dismissal by John McManus

Perfect Financial Ratios by Terry Gasking

The Perfect Interview by Max Eggert

Perfect Marketing by Louella Miles

The Perfect Meeting by David Sharman

The Perfect Negotiation by Gavin Kennedy

Perfect PR by Marie Jennings

Perfect Presentation by Andrew Leigh and Michael Maynard

Perfect Recruitment by David Oates and Viv Shackleton

The Perfect Report by Peter Bartram

The Perfect Sale by Nick Thornely and Dan Lees

Perfect Stress Control by Carole McKenzie

Perfect Teamwork by Ron Johnson

Perfect Time Management by Ted Johns

Perfect Freelancing

ALL YOU NEED
TO GET IT RIGHT
FIRST TIME

SEAN MARRIOTT and PAULA JACOBS

ARROW
BUSINESS BOOKS

Published by Arrow Books in 1995

1 3 5 7 9 10 8 6 4 2

Copyright © Sean Marriott and Paula Jacobs 1995

Sean Marriott and Paula Jacobs have asserted their rights under the Copyright, Designs and Patents Act, 1988, to be identified as the authors of this work.

This book is sold subject to the condition that it shall not, by way of trade or otherwise, be lent, resold, hired out, or otherwise circulated without the publisher's prior consent in any form of binding or cover other than that in which it is published and without a similar condition including this condition being imposed on the subsequent purchaser.

First published by
Arrow Books Limited
20 Vauxhall Bridge Road, London SW1V 2SA

Random House Australia (Pty) Limited
20 Alfred Street, Milsons Point, Sydney
New South Wales 2061, Australia

Random House New Zealand Limited
18 Poland Road, Glenfield
Auckland 10, New Zealand

Random House South Africa (Pty) Limited
PO Box 337, Bergvlei, South Africa

Random House UK Limited Reg. No. 954009

ISBN 0 09 950531 2

Set in Bembo by
SX Composing Ltd, Rayleigh, Essex
Printed and bound in Great Britain by
Cox & Wyman Ltd, Reading, Berkshire

British Library Cataloguing in Publication Data
A catalogue record for this book is available from
the British Library

For my parents (with thanks)
and Clair (without an 'e')
SM

For Dorothy and Frederick Jacobs, my parents
PJ

ACKNOWLEDGEMENTS

For their helpful insights: Dennis Barker; Lionel Browne; Ian Chapman; Margaret Collins; Simon Cuff; Nancy Duin; Paolo Francis; Mary Garnish; Richard Gillard; Ian Jones; Kate Kirkwood; Mike Kirkwood; Mark Marriott; Dave May; Mary Morton; Philip Morton; Reg Sammarco; Louise Spencely; Woodie Taylor; Edward Twentyman; Anne Yarwood.

Particular thanks, as ever, to Elizabeth Hennessy.

CONTENTS

Introduction xi

1. Getting Started 1

2. Culture Shocks 5

3. Using Advice 9

4. Where are my Clients? 12

5. CV or not CV 16

6. Business Stationery 26

7. Telephone Manners 29

8. The Client's Perspective 34

9. Negotiating Skills 42

10. Give me the Money! 49

11. Working From Home 57

12. Lifelines 66

13. Saying 'No' to Work 73

14. If Things Go Wrong 78

Appendix A   Tax & Legal 85

Appendix B   Contacts 92

INTRODUCTION

Whether you are considering a freelance career, have just started out, or are already working freelance, this book should have something to offer you.

Being a professional freelancer means being adaptable, single-minded and self-reliant, for which there are no set rules. So, despite its title, this book is not really about perfection. Our ideas and advice are intended to help you keep to your chosen path, rather than dictate a 'perfect' path which you should follow.

Neither are we selling the idea that you can 'get rich quick' if you read this book; that's up to you. Remember, you can't base a career on theory, and a neatly-typed business plan is no substitute for knowing what you want to do and sticking to it.

Freelancing is no easy option, but it does represent a liberating alternative for those of us who look for challenge, variety and flexibility in how we use our skills. We know of few who have tried it and gone back 'into the fold'.

Any comments or queries will be received with great interest. You can write to us c/o Arrow Books, Random House, 20 Vauxhall Bridge Road, London SW1V 2SA.

1
GETTING STARTED

WHAT IS A FREELANCER?
'A person, usually self-employed, who offers work or services to a variety of businesses and individuals without working on a regular salary basis for any one employer.'

WHAT ARE YOU GOING TO DO?
A great deal depends on your reasons for going freelance. While some people want to continue with the type of work they have done full-time, others will use the opportunity to develop by either specializing or diversifying.

If you have heavy financial commitments (mortgage, family etc) your approach to building a freelance career will obviously be inspired by your need for a regular income. Although this may appear to limit your options, you can still choose a starting point that leaves room for development as you progress.

WHAT DO YOU HAVE TO OFFER?
In order to establish yourself, how will you use your abilities to the greatest effect? Consider the following questions:

- What are your specific professional skills or areas of experience?
- Which of these are likely to be in the most demand?

You may find that the skills and experience that are most useful in the early stages of your freelance career do not necessarily reflect the status of your last full-time position. For instance:

Mr Font, senior manager in a typesetting firm, is made redundant when new technology renders many of the company's services obsolete. He invests in some of this new technology and sets up on his own.

He is no longer a manager of anyone but himself and must instead use all his old typing and layout skills (as well as answering the telephone and being his own teaboy).

Equally, you may find that freelancing will immediately give you an outlet for abilities that have hitherto been underused or not used at all.

Moira has been working as a secretary in a prestigious PR consultancy. Although she has studied PR and has vocational qualifications, the company favours university graduates of a certain background.

In her spare time she has put her knowledge and enthusiasm to good use, raising awareness for several community projects. Working alone, she has had to develop her skills in many different areas. She now has contacts in the local media (radio, newspapers etc) and has gained valuable experience.

She leaves to become freelance. Rather than having to wait several years to work on large company accounts, she can already offer a complete PR service to small businesses in her area.

CREATING A BALANCE

An approach somewhere between the two examples is probably the most likely. A point that we shall return to is the fact that your freelance work should reflect a balance between:

- what will guarantee a steady income; and
- what will create new opportunities.

Without the former, you will probably starve before

GETTING STARTED

you can make use of the latter. Equally, with no new challenges or opportunities your business cannot develop.

Whatever your circumstances or commitments it is important to create this balance.

WHY FREELANCING?

What are you looking for? Though not for everyone, freelancing can offer any or all of the following advantages:

- You should find greater variety and challenge in your working life.
- People are more likely to judge you on what you can do, not whether your face 'fits'.
- Experience seems to be more valued in freelancing; again, this comes down to what you can do.
- Discrimination on any number of grounds (age, sex, race, disability) becomes far less pronounced.
- You have the autonomy and flexibility to fit your work around other priorities and commitments.
- Your development is not at the mercy of company hierarchies or office politics, it is in your own hands.
- You are less likely to be pigeon-holed. ('Well that's not really your department, is it?')
- Improved communications technology means that many types of work can be done from almost anywhere.
- There is no compulsory retirement age.

Broadly speaking, freelancing represents freedom; *including* the freedom to sink or swim. It can have a great many advantages, but it will be up to you to make the most of them. How will you prepare for your new working life?

PERFECT FREELANCING

CHECKLIST
- Think about which of your skills are likely to be in the most demand.
- Consider how you will adapt to a new way of working.
- Balance work that gives a steady income with work that creates new opportunities.

2
CULTURE SHOCKS

The average full-time environment provides you with a fairly rigid framework in which to operate. By and large you know when you will be working and what you will be paid at the end of the month. You know what you're expected to do and even what you should wear. Ask yourself:

- To what extent are your organizational abilities or punctuality a product of your full-time routine?
- Once the routine disappears how self-disciplined will you be?

GOODBYE PERKS
As well as telling you what to do and when to do it, your old employers also provided a certain amount of support and one or two 'goodies'. Take into account that:

- Nobody will pay you for bank holidays (around eight a year), annual leave (15 – 25 working days) or time off sick. Over a year, this probably means losing between 25 and 30 days (five or six working weeks).
- It is unlikely that anyone will pay to send you on training courses or the like.
- You will only be paid for what you do; no more coasting through slack days.
- You are now responsible for all your administration; things like typing letters or sending out invoices and chasing them up.
- Tax and National Insurance contributions are now your responsibility. You may choose to employ an accountant, but still have to go to the trouble of keeping records.

ARE YOU ADAPTABLE?

If you come to freelancing from a longstanding full-time position, how set in your ways are you? Having followed a steady routine for some time you must now adjust to a new set of challenges and choices.

The key is to abandon your preconceptions of how you go about your work, or what is expected of you. As you will now be working for a number of different employers you must adapt to a variety of different requirements.

You may be doing the same work, but *how* it is done will vary with each individual client.

SELF-MOTIVATION

Many people prefer being flung headlong into work – the 'all hands to the pumps' approach – as it keeps them motivated.

If you find it difficult to focus your efforts without this impetus, will you have problems disciplining yourself when left to your own devices? Working on your own (probably at home) may mean you are too easily distracted from necessary, but uninspiring, jobs:

Simon (Actor/Voice Coach): My most common stumbling block is not having a boss to stand behind me cracking a big whip. Consequently, there's too much leeway for procrastination and not facing up to difficult issues.

Note: Our solution has been to take on this type of work only when it involves working in-house at the client's office. This way we are not distracted by supposedly better things to do with our time. The less diverted you are from the job, the quicker you can get it out of the way.

ARE YOU EASYGOING?

In a full-time environment many people feel that an easygoing attitude may undermine their position or professional credibility. In freelancing a calm, good-natured attitude is actually a huge asset; particularly in surviving highly pressurized or chaotic work situations.

Note: When you are dealing with new clients, a relaxed attitude can obscure your professionalism, if it is *too much* to the fore.

FROM MANAGER TO MINION

For anyone coming to freelancing from a managerial background there has to be a certain amount of re-adjustment. The same is true of more mature professionals with longstanding experience.

As well as sometimes taking on less challenging or prestigious work, you may also be working for somebody either younger or less experienced than you. Galling as this can be, always remember the following:

- Although you may be working for the client you are your own boss. The finer points of the work may be up to them but ultimate decisions about your career belong to you and not to an immediate superior or personnel director. (Overall, a promotion rather than a demotion, wouldn't you say?)
- A client may be only too aware of your greater experience or expertise and feel a defensive need to assert their authority all the more. You need to accept this for what it is and try not to react. If you appear understanding, and therefore less imposing, the client can stop feeling quite so defensive.

LOSING SOME CONTROL

If you are used to making decisions about the way work is done, how will you adapt to being a cog in someone else's machine?

In fact, it can be very liberating *not* to have overall responsibility. You can concentrate on your part of the work and leave the client to deal with all the peripheral complications (ie, they can do all the unpaid overtime and tear their hair out).

HOW WILL YOU ADAPT?
Being adaptable is important, but trying to be all things to all people will just create awkward compromises. Stick to your strengths, but learn to apply them to each new set of demands.

THE CHOICE IS YOURS
Ultimately, as a freelancer, you always have the option of saying 'No' to work, something it is difficult to do as a full-time employee. For this reason it's advisable to cultivate a number of clients, even if some of them aren't your first choice or don't pay that well.

(This is also important for establishing your tax status as self-employed; covered more fully in Appendix A 'Tax & Legal'.)

Remember: The psychological benefit of knowing that you *do* have a choice is a greater advantage than constantly exercising that choice. Creating and sustaining working relationships is vitally important.

CHECKLIST
- You will be losing a full-time routine and will need more self-discipline.
- You will no longer be paid for *any* time off.
- You may lose a prestigious job title, but you will gain autonomy.
- Stick to what you're good at, but learn to adapt how you do it.

3
USING ADVICE

As soon as people know you are contemplating a major change (becoming freelance, for instance) they will all want to give you the benefit of their experience.

Being receptive to new ideas will give you more choice than ignoring them; but how do you know which advice to take?

WHY ARE THEY TELLING ME THIS?
Whose interests or priorities does the advice most obviously represent, the adviser's or yours?

- Are they trying to sell you something? ('Of course you'll be needing to open a business account with us, won't you?' 'Well, nobody will take you seriously without a mobile phone.')
- Do they misguidedly feel they have your best interests at heart? ('Wouldn't you be better off with a steady job?' 'You'll never make money drawing pictures.')
- Do they see you as competition? ('Well I don't want to put you off, but . . .')
- Do they want you to rely on them? ('Of course, you're going to need a lot of help with this . . .')
- Are they parading their vast experience by being dismissive or cynical? ('They all say that to start off with . . .')

We are by no means suggesting that you automatically mistrust every helpful soul who offers advice, merely that you accept it in the right context.

TOO MANY COOKS
Even following all the sound advice you get can be confusing. You may get trapped amid a collection of plausible, but conflicting, directions:

'Too many cooks spoil the broth . . .'
but 'Many hands make light work . . .'

'Don't look a gift horse in the mouth'
but 'Beware of Greeks bearing gifts.'

Nobody can make up your mind for you. The advice is only as good as its relevance to your needs or personality. Do you know what you want, or what you are prepared to do in order to achieve it?

GOOD ADVICE

What the freelancers were told

Woodie (Drummer/Programmer): 'You're being employed to be you, don't try to be anybody else!'
Simon (Actor/Voice Coach): 'Do it for yourself.'
Mike & Kate (Publishing Services): One of our clients once said – *half*-jokingly, maybe – that we were 'almost professional'. That made us try a bit harder.
Anne (Counsellor): 'Assume your mantle', in other words accept your responsibility and use your talents.
Liz (Researcher): 'Ensure that deadline and payment arrangements are absolutely clear from the start.'
Mary (Production Editor): 'Get an answering machine.'
Ian (Graphic Designer): 'Get computerized before you're left behind.'

BAD ADVICE

What the freelancers were told

Simon (Actor/Voice Coach): 'Why don't you get a safe, steady job?'
Anne (Counsellor): 'A woman's place is in the home.'
Richard (Photographer): Many years ago, someone told me

that the only way I would sell my work was via an established picture agency ... like his, for instance! Despite his greater experience and success I knew that was not what I wanted. In fact, I just set up one of my own and carried on regardless.

Many (Production Editor): ... from my pensions adviser!

Ian (Graphic Designer): A telesales rep who said, 'You'll pick up a fair bit of work if you put an ad in our directory.'

PAYING FOR PROFESSIONAL ADVICE

It is tempting to approach someone with a clutch of half-formed ideas and expect them to sort everything out. As we have already established, it is up to you to decide what you need or are trying to achieve.

Think carefully through what you need first and try to work out what you can do for yourself. This will help you to pinpoint what you actually need to ask to get worthwhile answers. (Bear in mind that you will probably be charged by the hour, so don't waste any time.)

CHECKLIST

- Work out what you really want before taking advice on how to get it.
- Be receptive to advice, but be discerning as to its origin.
- Use advice to help achieve *your* aims, rather than mould yourself round other people's expectations.
- Don't use advice blindly, apply it to your own knowledge and experience.
- If you are using professional advice prepare beforehand. What do you actually need to know?

4
WHERE ARE MY CLIENTS?

Having given some thought to what you are going to do, who do you envisage doing it for? Some people have a lot of useful contacts, but others feel they have none at all. If you fall into the latter category, don't worry, you may find that you are not so alone as you thought.

THE OLD FIRM
At one company we were involved with it became a running joke that every redundant manager was invited to come back on a 'consultancy' basis.

Many companies are rather more bashful about using ex-employees as freelance workers. Perhaps they are embarrassed, or assume that ex-staff members will hurl a spanner in the works during a fit of embittered rage.

Nevertheless, colleagues and work contacts can be a good place to start when targeting your own clients. They will know you and probably be in the line of work you intend to pursue. Obviously, much depends on the circumstances of your departure. Understandably, many people want to make a clean break and start afresh.

CONTACTS AND PERSONAL RECOMMENDATION
In the course of your work you may well have had dealings with people from other companies in a similar field. These could be suppliers or complementary businesses and, even, competitors. (The latter may be particularly keen to avail themselves of your experience . . .)

We have yet to meet a freelancer (including actors, designers, musicians, illustrators, writers and photographers) who has not emphasized the value of personal recommendation.

This does not mean that you can't get on if you don't know anyone useful. The news is somewhat better than that; if you do a successful job for one client there is a good chance they will recommend you to other people. Your first few clients are crucial in that respect.

In the same way that theatrical projects or music tours often warm up in the provinces, you may need the opportunity to hone your skills and gain experience with smaller jobs. You will then be better placed to succeed with more important clients.

ADVERTISING

We have so far not really come across any freelancers for whom general advertising, in newspapers or magazines, has been a successful or cost-effective means of targeting clients. You will probably find that using methods of promotion which allow you to target more directly will be of most use.

However, recruitment advertising for full-time staff can be very revealing as to the nature and needs of the business involved.

It often provides you with a relevant contact name and number. Using freelance support could be an option that they have not yet considered. If nothing else, this means you will not be competing with a legion of other hungry freelancers.

TRADE DIRECTORIES

These can work for you in one of two ways:

- advertising your services to a specific market; and
- providing you with a detailed list of potential clients.

Given their shelf life (generally a year) these can be a

cost-effective way of advertising yourself. Their weakness may be that your entry appears among a mass of other people offering much the same thing.

The key here is to analyse what else is on offer and see how you can differentiate your service, perhaps by combining certain skills or emphasizing others. What is on offer remains the same, but how it is presented attracts attention.

PJ: When giving details to a trade directory I focused on certain skills that I noticed had not been highlighted in other people's entries. In the index of skills at the back of the new directory, mine was the only name under certain categories. This brought in a number of new clients.

A directory will also allow you to focus your attention on the clients who are most likely to need your services. Often, relevant contact names are included along with the address and telephone number.

Local libraries are usually well stocked with a variety of trade directories. This saves you having to invest anything between £20 and £100 a copy.

WHAT DO YOU CHARGE?

Having gone to the trouble of attracting clients, you will need to know how much to charge for your work.

Companies who are used to dealing with freelancers probably have a set rate, anyway. If you begin by targeting these, you get to learn what people will pay and what factors influence different rates (urgency, unsocial hours etc). When you come to negotiate with new clients, you then have a much better idea of what your skills are worth.

Another way of setting your charges is to find out

standard rates from a relevant trade organization. (As writers and editors, we could establish a rough pricing policy based on NUJ rates, for instance.)

Beyond this it's a question of what you can get. Chapter 9 'Negotiating Skills' takes this a step further and looks at the other issues you will want to take into account.

CHECKLIST
- You may have something to offer existing contacts.
- Your first few clients are crucial as they can spread the word.
- If you do a good job for one client they can recommend you to their colleagues.
- Use less important clients to build experience.
- Use companies' recruitment advertising for full-time staff as a way of establishing their freelance needs.
- If you advertise in a trade directory try to differentiate your service from others in the same field.
- Use your local library for research.
- Working for clients with set rates will give you a rough idea of your market value.
- A relevant trade association can also guide you on pricing.

5
CV OR NOT CV

In certain professions, it is possible to demonstrate examples of your work to prospective clients rather than merely listing your abilities:

- A portfolio of work for artists, architects, designers etc.
- A showreel for anyone working in television, video or film.
- A demo tape for radio broadcasters, voice-over artists, musicians etc.

If this list covers your chosen freelance career you will be familiar with these approaches. Nevertheless, much of the general advice that follows would be applicable, as the issues remain the same:

- Whichever medium you use to showcase your skills, don't let yourself down with poor presentation.
- Make sure that anything you send has a contact name and telephone number on it.
- Be conscious of what will be of interest to the client and don't obscure this with irrelevancies.

WHAT TO INCLUDE

The traditional form of a CV, which might include everything from your participation in team sports to your keen interest in basket-weaving, is not really relevant to freelancing.

Prospective clients need something that tells them about you, and they tend to call it 'a CV'. What *we* would actually send covers the following:

- areas of experience and other clients;

- details of on-site equipment;
- relevant training and qualifications;
- address, telephone/fax numbers etc.

AREAS OF EXPERIENCE AND OTHER CLIENTS

The crux of the matter. Clients need to know that you can do their work, their way; everything else is distinctly secondary.

Straight from full-time employment

Try to focus on the areas of experience most relevant to prospective clients' likely needs. A lot of the high falutin' baggage accumulated in office hierarchies means little in the outside world.

For instance, management ability (or even experience of dealing with your own freelancers) is only relevant as a tool to convince clients that you understand *their* needs and priorities. Unless management skills are a specific prerequisite, over-emphasizing that point can do little more than intimidate prospective clients.

Always adopt the traditional CV practice of working in a reverse chronology, putting most recent work first. If you can put areas of experience under different headings, do this within each area. You can then put the most relevant area of experience first.

With a few existing clients

You will want to create a coherent image of what you have done for other people and what, by implication, you can do for the client. You can mention other clients, their line of business, which of your skills were utilized and how. Within the confines of the job, what did you achieve on the client's behalf?

Again, use areas of experience as categories and, where possible, put those most relevant to the prospective client in the most prominent position.

ON-SITE EQUIPMENT

Any equipment that highlights your accessibility – fax, modem, or even an answering machine – will increase your appeal. As one client put it: 'They can reduce some of the disadvantages which result from not having someone working in the office next to you.'

Even without a fax of your own, most small print shops/office suppliers offer some kind of service for receiving incoming transmissions. It's always worth mentioning that access to this service is available.

In certain areas the other main issue is compatibility. With everything from text and illustrations to music and moving images being captured on computer disk, system compatibility can make the difference between getting or losing a job.

Don't, however, go into a wealth of unnecessary detail, stick to whatever is relevant to the work at hand. You can always be more specific later on.

Another by-product of this may be that clients give you greater credibility:

Leonard (Production Manager): Equipment is proof to me that people are serious about their work, because they need to recoup the financial outlay.

ADDRESS AND TELEPHONE/FAX NUMBERS

Again, highlight your accessibility if possible; if you are close to the client's premises, nearest big town, main-line stations and main roads. Give details of location (and a map if relevant) for courier services.

Make sure your telephone number is prominent because it allows people to get into immediate and direct contact with you.

TRAINING AND QUALIFICATIONS

Do make reference to a *relevant* trade qualification or degree; both of which may be signalled merely by including appropriate letters after your name.

A degree presupposes a certain level of success at A/O level or GCSE standard, so there is really no need to include further details.

In any event, for anyone over 25 years old secondary school qualifications seem ever more remote and irrelevant. Clients will be far more interested in your experience or examples of your work.

Note: Many full-time job advertisements automatically ask for a degree, whether entirely relevant or not, as a means of pre-sorting a flood of applications. With freelancers far less emphasis is placed on paper qualifications, all that should matter is whether you can do the work or not.

WHAT YOU CAN LEAVE OUT

You will notice that we have not included any of the following:

- date of birth;
- secondary education details (see 'Training and Qualifications' above)
- positions of responsibility in the community;
- leisure interests;
- personal details (marital status, family, race or sexual orientation).

Although these are prominent questions on most job application forms, and huge blank spaces are left for you to fill in, they are not that relevant when you're freelance.

Date of birth

CV experts generally suggest that if you omit your age it will be assumed that you are hiding something (perhaps the shocking truth that you are over 30).

Where freelancing is concerned this should not really be an issue. Obviously, areas of work influenced by trends and fads (for instance, fashion, or some areas of graphic design and journalism) may have certain image requirements. Even then, a lot depends of how 'visible' you are.

Allow prospective clients to see what you can do for them before they need to worry about your age.

Positions of responsibility in the community
A full-time employer may need to know that they are taking an eminently responsible, trustworthy type on to their staff but a client may not even have to have you on the premises. If they don't trust you they don't have to use you again, or at all . . . simple as that.

If, however, you hold some kind of office that would have a specific bearing on your work it is quite legitimate to mention it.

Leisure interests
Clients just need a job done, they are not employing you to have cosy chats about your stamp collection.

Where this does become relevant is if the combination of your professional expertise and private interests is of some use to the client. If you are a current affairs copywriter, but have a passion for fishing, your hobby could be more relevant than your professional speciality to someone on a fishing magazine.

Equally, if your freelance work would require a degree of physical fitness it would be appropriate to mention any athletic or sporting activities.

Personal details
If you can do the job, nobody's business but your own, we say. Female freelancers shouldn't have to suffer the

usual employer trepidation about their family planning, because clients are not liable for maternity payments. Anything else is irrelevant, unless it relates directly to the work that the client is offering.

JUST ENOUGH BUT NO MORE

You are telling the prospective client *just enough* to arouse their interest. If they want to know more they can always ask you. Including a lot of irrelevant facts merely dilutes your appeal.

Yes, but what did you actually do?

It is easy to write down a full-time job title and responsibilities, but prospective clients will be more interested in what you actually *did*. If possible, include the basic details first and present your achievements in a list underneath.

The big 'I' am

> 'Well that's enough about me,
> tell me about yourself . . .
> What do *you* think of me?'

Cobwebby jokes aside, how do you sell yourself without appearing boastful or egocentric? By definition, you must talk favourably about yourself and your achievements.

The answer is to avoid the use of 'I' wherever possible. By following the pattern outlined above, and presenting your achievements as a list, this is not difficult.

'While involved in the project I was able to:

- cut costs;
- train staff;
- introduce a new system of . . . '

How long?

Keep it short. One A4 page (210 × 297mm) is as much as most people will read thoroughly, hence our emphasis on presenting only relevant information.

UPDATING

Do not get too many spare copies of your freelance CV at first. As you get established in your freelance work you will be able to improve it constantly by adding clients, skills and jobs as they come along.

Do not hesitate to send an updated version to someone if you've added new information which you think they will find relevant.

PRESENTING YOUR CV

It goes without saying that your CV should be typed or word processed (unless there is a specific reason for having it handwritten). Quite aside from giving a more professional appearance, this makes it much easier to update quickly or move material around.

Try not to use standard photocopier paper which is quite flimsy and puts across a rather cheap image. Stationers and copy shops will all have a selection of heavier 100gsm paper (standard photocopier paper is only 80gsm). This still passes quite happily through most photocopiers and gives a far more polished and substantial look.

Initially, you can't go wrong using plain white paper. As you progress you may want to experiment or keep it consistent with your other business stationery.

Check spelling

Having tried to put across a competent, professional image of yourself it would be a shame to be let down by something as easily avoided as spelling mistakes.

Check what you have written, twice if possible, and ask someone else to have a look through it as well. Check the grammar and use short, punchy sentences.

Covering letters
Your covering letter is merely there to encourage the client to read your CV. Briefly say who you are and why you are sending them your details. Finish with an offer to provide any other information they might need or discuss things further in a meeting.

What you must establish as quickly as possible is a connection between what they may need and what you can provide. This should signal the fact that you already have some knowledge and understanding of who they are and what they do. For the same reason, always write to them by name; ring the company to check this and get details of correct spellings and job titles.

FOLLOW-UP TELEPHONE CALL
Ring people up a couple of days after you have sent your details, in order to check they have arrived. You can also take this opportunity to remind them that you can provide any further information they need and are available to meet them.

Making verbal contact is important to keep you at the front of their mind. It also allows them to know a little more about you, so that you become less of an unknown quantity. Be polite and friendly, don't put them under pressure or sound too desperate.

If you can't get through to the person you need to speak to, don't be impatient with whoever has answered the phone. The opinion *they* form will be passed on with the message.

CVs

What the clients say

Louise (Editorial Services Manager): CVs are of limited use, but they are the only way I can tell if people have the skills and expertise that I am looking for. If they don't send in a CV, just a brief letter containing very little information (which quite often happens), they won't get a second look.

Edward (Freelance Agency): The worst are these ones designed by consultancies who sell you a CV... They look terribly impressive if you don't know anything about it, but they're not helpful. They conceal far more than they reveal, because they're written by somebody who doesn't really know you and puts in what he thinks are good CV-type phrases like 'an experienced manager with good person power'.

Donald (Art Director): CVs are not terribly useful, but often a first line of attack. When building a team of like-minded people, the only sure method is to interview the candidate.

Margaret (Educational Training): I never look at them! Trainers are often referred to me from another part of the department. Other times, I see someone speaking whose style I like and who I could feel comfortable working with. I can usually tell from speaking to someone on the phone whether they will work out or not.

Jan (Commissions Photographers): Written details are not relevant, we just need to see their work.

Leonard (Production Manager): You need to know what a freelancer is *demonstrably* good at. Look *first* at what they do now, then at their background.

CHECKLIST
- Clients need to know what you can do for them; arrange your CV to show this.
- Make sure your CV includes relevant experience, other clients, on-site equipment, appropriate training and qualifications.
- Don't oversell yourself, or appear over-qualified.
- Put the most relevant work first.
- On-site equipment highlights your accessibility.

- Make sure that *anything* you send has your name and telephone number on it.
- Highlight information which will arouse their interest and don't bore them with irrelevant details.
- Avoid the use of 'I' as much as possible.
- Pay attention to presentation, keep it short, keep it up to date.
- Use good quality paper (100gsm).

6
BUSINESS STATIONERY

Every time you post a letter or send a fax you are promoting an image of yourself and your business. Your stationery should therefore reflect the care and professionalism which you apply to your work.

WHO ARE YOU?
As a sole trader you can use a trade name if you want; although you must still include your own name on your business stationery. You are not allowed to use words like: Limited, plc, Royal, Trust, Association; or anything that may be considered offensive.

The trade name or description of your service should be general enough to accommodate any development you might have in mind, eg 'Photographic Services' rather than 'Wedding Photographer'.

DESIGN
Naturally you want to promote the right image – professional, reliable, outstandingly efficient – but you also have to keep within a budget.

The key here is to keep things simple. In particular, avoid using umpteen typefaces or trying to turn your name into a clever representation of what you do.

HEADED PAPER
A good way of getting off on the right foot with whoever you contact. A little care and thought at the design stage can help you to convey a degree of respectability and professionalism.

You will, as with the CV, be looking for 100gsm paper. Many of the small print shops around only stock white and off-white nowadays, although they can order coloured paper in.

Note: Small print shops are not necessarily any better qualified than you are to design letter headings etc. If in doubt, keep it simple.

Faxing or photocopying

How well will your headed paper transmit as a fax or reproduce on a photocopier? With type that is too small or thin the results may become illegible. If it is on heavily tinted paper it may well reproduce as an indistinct grey blob, and lighter coloured inks may be lost altogether.

COMPLIMENT SLIPS

These can be remarkably useful if much of your correspondence is short comments (perhaps accompanying posted work or the like). They come in a variety of shapes and sizes, but are probably at their most versatile measuring 210mm × 99mm, conveniently one third of an A4 sheet.

They should be printed with your name/company name, address and telephone/fax details. (You can add the words 'with compliments', if you want to be literal about it.)

As well as being cost-effective (you get three on an A4 sheet) they also encourage quicker, less formal messages.

BUSINESS CARDS

These are most useful as a quick way of telling someone who you are, what you do and where you can be contacted. Many people automatically get cards printed, but end up hardly using any. Do you really need them?

Consider the following before deciding:

- In the first instance will you generally be approaching prospective clients via an introductory letter?
- How many contacts are you likely to be making at trade fairs etc, or in social settings such as restaurants and bars where business cards would be useful?
- What do *you* do with other people's business cards?

QUANTITIES

If you are not planning to move in the near future 300–500 cards or sheets of headed paper are most economical. Because a fair proportion of costs (making printing plates etc) are fixed whatever the quantity, the difference in price between 200 and 300 say, is negligible. (You may be doing a blanket mailing to 100 prospective clients to get started anyway.)

Note: As ever, try to get more than one quote.

RECYCLED PAPER

Recycling is good for your image and the environment, but this has to be balanced against presentation. We would advise always making first contact with a new client on good quality paper, using a fresh envelope.

CHECKLIST

- Use business stationery to promote the right image.
- You can use a trade name, but must include your own name somewhere on the stationery.
- Keep designs simple.
- Ensure that your headed paper will reproduce clearly as a photocopy or a fax.
- The difference in price between printing 200 and 300 of anything is negligible because of fixed costs (printing plates etc); 300–500 copies are usually most economical.
- Get more than one quote.

7
TELEPHONE MANNERS

One way or another, you will be spending much more time on the telephone. As well as selling off vital organs to pay the bill, you will also need to be more conscious of how you project yourself. What these tips set out to do is help you feel at ease with whoever you deal with.

If you are poorly prepared or plagued with interruptions it is hard to give of your best. Developing confidence, with a few guidelines to fall back on, makes it a lot easier to be yourself.

BE PREPARED
If it is a new client or an important issue you wish to discuss, do think about what you want to say, and what you *don't* want to say. (Keep a list in front of you if this will help.) This way you won't be drawn into irrelevancies or issues that may undermine what you want to achieve. You will also sound more organized and are less likely to waste time.

WHEN TO CALL
It's better to phone people:

- in the morning – they've got all day to do what you want;
- just after lunch – with some food inside them most people are more amenable;
- early in the week – stake your claim before a load of other priorities are commanding their attention.

Potentially bad times to call are:

- just before lunch – they won't have the patience to pay much attention if they are desperate for a break;

- at the end of the day – the last thing they want is to be held up when they are trying to get away from the office.

GATEKEEPERS

If you are dealing with someone's secretary or assistant be aware of the following:

- Don't be condescending – it is unwise to make assumptions about their status.
- Don't try to sound important or imposing by being terse with them – rudeness is unprofessional full stop.

They may well be in a position of some influence, and are usually able to tell you much of what you need to know, for instance:

- Whether you are wasting your time – is the person you are trying to contact the one you actually need to speak to?
- What the prospective client's likely needs or priorities are – after all, they work with them.

Remember: Anyone you speak to at a client company can pass on an opinion of you with the message. Make sure you leave them with a good impression. Also make a note of their name, as you may well be speaking to them again.

DON'T BE A PARROT

Whether through a lack of self-confidence or a misguided attempt at bonding with a client, don't be tempted to change the way you speak. It is likely you will modify your language, depending on the level of your conversation, but adopting the other person's vocal mannerisms means that you just sound like a parrot.

By all means show that you understand or agree, 'Yes, I see', but try not to repeat back what they have said verbatim.

SM: I finished a call and a colleague said 'That was the printer on the phone, wasn't it?' I asked how she knew from the little I had said. 'Well, you had your patronizing "lawd luv us I'm just like one of you..." accent on' she replied.

WE CAN HEAR YOU...
Should your conversation inspire you to give an elated cry of '*Yes* . . . I've got it!' or a frustrated 'what a berk . . .' remember to say this *after* you have put the phone right down. Just because you have said 'goodbye' and taken the receiver from your ear does not mean that they have stopped listening at the other end.

Sticking your hand over the mouthpiece while you comment on the call to somebody else ('Don't worry, I'll soon get rid of him . . .') is also risky.

QUIET PLEASE
Ideally, if you are working from home you do need to isolate yourself, so that your business calls will be uninterrupted. Where small children are concerned this is not always easy. If there is a child screaming in the background it is *not* the end of the world; it is usually when parents scream back that it becomes a little off-putting!

WHO'S THERE?
Try to automatically answer the phone as if it is a client on the other end. Assuming it is a friend who promised to call back and greeting them with 'Hello, Trumpton Fire Station, Captain Flack speaking' will probably put you on the wrong foot with a new client.

Be friendly but professional: 'Hello, can I help you?'

This not only puts across a more efficient image, but also helps you to feel more businesslike.

ANSWERING MACHINES

Generally accepted as one of the more useful pieces of freelance equipment. They emphasize your accessibility by making you appear available even when you're not.

What to look for

Different models offer all sorts of impressive-sounding features, but the following are probably the most important:

- **Call screening** – If you leave your answering machine on so that you are not interrupted, you can still hear who is on the line and pick up if it is urgent.
- **Remote control** – If you want to check for messages while you are out, some models provide a gadget which activates the playback of your messages down the telephone line to wherever you are.

Your outgoing message

Unless you have a model with a built-in 'robot' message, you will be recording one of your own. What do you say?

'We're sorry there's no one available to take your call at the moment. Please leave a message after the tone and we will get back to you as soon as possible.'

The use of the royal 'we', even if you are on your own, seems to create a more rounded, less lonely, image. For women freelancers it can also be a way of deterring nuisance callers, who may otherwise prey on their apparent isolation.

You need to sound approachable as well as businesslike, but bear the following in mind:

- **Avoid long messages** – They merely waste other people's time and run up their phone bills. Say what you have to then give the caller a chance to leave their message.
- **Don't try to be too perky** – Indiscriminate chirpiness becomes irritating after repetition, particularly if someone is having difficulty getting hold of you. You don't have to speak in a dull monotone, just be clear and straightforward.
- **Don't try to be funny** – In-jokes with friends are all very well, but how do you know if prospective clients will share your sense of humour? (The joke will also wear thin pretty quickly.)
- **Avoid using music** – There used to be a fad for using background music on messages, but the end results were less than impressive. Bearing in mind the distinctly 'lo-fi' quality of recording, *and* the fact that it will be played back down a telephone line, this approach is not recommended.

CHECKLIST
- Prepare for calls; know what you want to say.
- Call people when they are likely to be at their best; morning or early afternoon.
- Don't be patronizing or overbearing when dealing with secretaries or assistants, be professional.
- Anyone you leave messages with will pass on their impression with that message.
- Note the name of anybody you leave a message with.
- Put the phone *right down* before saying anything you don't want the other person to hear.
- Try to isolate yourself from interruptions.
- An answering machine makes you appear more accessible.
- Keep your outgoing messages short and simple.

8
THE CLIENT'S PERSPECTIVE

There is more to freelance work than just being good at your job. You also need to cooperate with your clients and inspire their confidence in you.

There may be no contact at all between you from the beginning of the job to the end. Your client must be able to trust you to get on with the work the way they want it done; not take up their time with trivial queries, but ring alarm bells immediately if it's justified.

In order to achieve all this you must develop an understanding of your client's perspective.

WHY USE FREELANCERS?

Louise (Editorial Services Manager): We can cope with variations in workload much more easily when using freelance staff. We also have access to a wide variety of different skills, which it would be impossible to have using only in-house staff.

As we have already seen, clients are only indirectly responsible for your overheads (these are absorbed into what they pay you) and they do not have to pay you for time off.

Your services will also represent a resource that they can call upon as and when they need it.

YOUR CLIENT'S PRIORITIES

Practically every client that we have ever had has valued flexibility and the ability to meet deadlines above all else. Impeccable credentials or brilliant technical skills come to mean very little if they can't be applied to the job in hand, in the time allotted.

Be flexible enough to help the client get the end result they want, rather than the one you feel (in your professional wisdom) they ought to have.

What about your professional pride, or credibility?

> 'Never seem more learned than the people you are with. Wear your learning like a pocket-watch and keep it hidden. Do not pull it out to count the hours, but give the time when you are asked.'
> *Philip Dormer Stanhope*

This does not mean that in order to get on you must make endless compromises or be happy to do a shoddy job, far from it. If you feel that a client's requirements are unreasonable or unrealistic, and have facts to back this up, you should say so; *how* you do it is most important.

In general, asking a question 'Do you think that . . . ?' is the best way to query the client's instructions. It gets them thinking about why they want something done and allows them to discuss it without losing face.

Simply telling someone 'If you do that it won't work' is not advisable. They are more likely to react by defending their opinion or attacking yours than by changing their mind.

BRIEFING
There is more to briefing than just letting the client tell you what to do.

Do you know what the client wants?
Make sure that you are clear from the outset as to what is expected of you. Even in the same professions, many people use different terminology. You can clarify *what*

the client wants done by using questions, for instance: 'So you're looking for someone to . . . ?' This also encourages the client to say *how* they want things done: 'Don't do it good, do it Thursday.'

Does the client know what the client wants?

Part of your job may be to help the client decide what they want. Try to establish their overall aims and then suggest alternative ways that you could contribute.

Often, clients will only arrive at what they are really looking for by exploring what they *don't* want. Frustrating as this may be, it is better to find out as early as possible.

A young designer was asked to create an album cover for a well-known rock band. The album had no title and the musicians were unable to offer any more detailed requirements than wanting a 'sweaty, South American feel'. The designer worked to the brief as diligently and imaginatively as he could and presented the results . . . which were rejected.

Another designer was used and the album eventually appeared with a blurry photograph of children's toys on the cover. Neither 'sweaty' nor 'South American' it suggested that the band had needed some experimentation before they knew what they *really* wanted.

GUIDING THE CLIENT

Ultimately the right way to do a job is the client's way. Nevertheless, if you have a client who is not sure what they want, or doesn't understand what you do, how do you guide them? In short, tactfully and professionally. (For an example, see Chapter 14 'If Things Go Wrong'.)

If the client cannot afford to be sensitive to the finer points, try to accept this. By all means make suggestions, but don't harangue them into accepting your expert views on how the job should be done.

THE PART YOU PLAY

Remember to see your role in context. Depending on the nature of the work, your tasks and deadlines will often be determined by what comes before and after your involvement. With this in mind, be conscious of the following:

- Avoid carelessly missing deadlines, thereby creating a more difficult schedule for whoever works on the next part of the process.
- Don't bolster your own efforts by deliberately highlighting shortcomings in previous stages of the work.

Also be aware that inconsiderate types (who obviously haven't read this book) may do the same to you. Be warned.

'US AND THEM ...'

Get any group of freelancers together and the conversation turns around to 'Them' at some point. That is, the disparate group of people who change their requirements half way through a job, demand the impossible and take two months of badgering before they pay up because they can't communicate properly with their own accounts department.

These are the clients, trapped in their routines, accountable for every penny of their budget to some psychotic superior who is armed with a sharp knife and an IOU for several pounds of flesh. Hmmmm . . .

Well, convincing yourself that full-timers are sad unimaginative no-hopers (while you are some kind of enviable 'free spirit') may make you feel jolly important but will do little for your working relationships with them.

The more interest you take in your client and their

work, the more you will understand about their priorities and the pressures they are under. This will be invaluable to you in judging what factors are important and doing the job the client wants.

Note: Ultimately, you should try to view your clients as colleagues.

GETTING TO KNOW YOU

Many freelancers never actually meet their clients. If the work is straightforward and meetings or briefings are unnecessary it is easy for this to happen. Nevertheless, face to face you usually get a much clearer and franker idea of what clients are looking for.

Working in-house gives you a better understanding of the process you are a part of. You can become more aware of clients' priorities by being involved in their working environment (the pressures they are under and the people they work with). You are also more visible to their colleagues as a potential freelance resource and known quantity. This applies equally to delivering or collecting work in person.

WHAT MAKES IT WORK?

From the client's perspective

Jan (Commissions Photographers): We regard the industry as 'our industry' and we're not really in the habit of trying to nail people to the floor, because we're all in the same business.

Louise (Editorial Services Manager): Professional skills, good communication and interpersonal abilities, notifying us if a deadline is going to be missed, dealing with people tactfully . . . Getting on, on a personal level, is also very important.

Edward (Freelance Agency): There must be mutual respect which comes from recognition of each other's competence and skill. To be a successful freelancer a person needs a certain robustness of character. They need to be able to speak their piece with courtesy but firmness.

THE CLIENT'S PERSPECTIVE

Margaret (Educational Training): Good interpersonal skills. People who are flexible and who do the job I need them to do.

Leonard (Production Manager): We want another version of us, who can just get on with the work. Both sides should be able to feel part of a team. A good working relationship is always important.

Elaine (Commissioning Editor): Flexibility and accessibility are important.

Donald (Art Director): I prefer freelance staff who solve the problems themselves, or present me with an alternative solution when jobs don't work out as planned.

From the freelancer's perspective

Ian (Graphic Designer): Making sure they always know they'll receive a good standard of service . . . and me not having to chase payments.

Anne (Counsellor): Openness, humour, straight talk and a non-judgmental attitude.

Paolo (Illustrator/Fine Artist): Understanding clients' needs and the ability to communicate, negotiate, compromise, persuade, trust, meet deadlines and deliver new ideas on demand.

Philip (Advertising/Direct Mail): There has to be flexibility on *both* sides.

Nancy (Writer/Editor): Keep in touch with the client. If a problem arises, tell them as soon as possible, rather than hoping it will go away. I find this very hard to do, even after 15 years as a freelancer.

Woodie (Drummer/Programmer): . . . probably my easy-going nature.

Simon (Actor/Voice Coach): Buckets of flattery and charm . . . finding out as precisely as possible what the client wants and raising all the sweat at your disposal to deliver it.

PERFECT FREELANCING

WHAT CLIENTS DON'T WANT

Louise (Editorial Services Manager): Problems have resulted from freelancers not wanting to work to the systems that we had set up, and not communicating with us enough (dates were missed and we weren't told) ... not being able to deal with people tactfully.

Edward (Freelance Agency): Somebody who's going to expect to have their nose wiped for them at every turn might do a very good job, but isn't going to be a great success as a freelancer.

Margaret (Educational Training): I have had problems with freelance trainers who are dogmatic or inflexible. If someone is employed to speak on a particular subject, but then insists on getting onto their own hobby-horse, this is no help to me or the trainees.

Leonard (Production Manager): Some freelancers just play at it. They only want to do certain types of work.

Elaine (Commissioning Editor): People who fail to observe deadlines or work slowly and push the price of the project up as a result.

CHECKLIST

- Clients value flexibility and the ability to meet deadlines very highly.
- Understanding your client's priorities helps you do the job they want, so take an interest.
- Try to treat your clients like colleagues.
- Be flexible enough to help the client get the end result they want, rather than the one you feel they ought to have.
- This does not mean that you must make endless compromises or be happy to do a shoddy job.
- Don't simply tell a client they are wrong; instead, ask a question that will highlight the problem and help them to work it out for themselves.
- Ultimately the right way to do a job is the client's way.

THE CLIENT'S PERSPECTIVE

- Be confident enough to accept when your expert opinion may not be needed.
- Remember to see your role in context as part of a wider process.
- Working in-house gives you a much clearer idea of clients' priorities.

9
NEGOTIATING SKILLS

Whenever you are discussing what a job will involve, the way in which it is to be done or what it is worth, you are negotiating.

Nevertheless, in the same way that chatting with a friend in your office does not really constitute being 'in a meeting', not every job discussion with a client has to become a negotiation.

Companies who use freelancers regularly tend to have a set hourly rate or flat fee for particular jobs. They also have some idea of how a job will be done and roughly how long it will take.

It is therefore not necessary to go through the full rigmarole every time someone rings you up with some work, a simple yes or no will do.

WHEN TO NEGOTIATE
There will be room for negotiation where the situation is more open-ended, for example:

- with a new client;
- with a 'one-off';
- when establishing the basis for a long-term freelance commitment;
- when there are special circumstances; or
- where specialist skills are required.

Remember: At the root of every negotiation will be the questions:

- How much do you need the client?
- How much does the client need you?

WHAT DO YOU CHARGE?

As we said in Chapter 4 'Where are my Clients?' you can base your charges initially on standard rates from a relevant trade organization, or on a going rate calculated from what other clients pay you for similar work.

Where there is no set rate, try to get some idea of the client's available budget. From there you can work out what you would be prepared to do for the money.

Getting clients to give you a figure can sometimes be nigh on impossible. They don't want to give too much away, any more than you would want to sell yourself short.

Clients with little experience of freelancers can be particularly awkward to negotiate with. Working for someone who does not know the market value of what you do hardly ever works in your favour. They tend to automatically assume that you will try to take advantage of them.

PRICING

What the freelancers say

Simon (Actor/Voice Coach): For creative work I consider the size of the work; how long it will take; whether I have worked for the people before and for how much; the amount of prestige involved or creative satisfaction to be derived (which might justify a lower fee).

Ian (Graphic Designer): The size of the company and the urgency of the job (what the market will bear). When quoting for design consultancies, printers etc, I have a standard generally accepted hourly rate.

Mike & Kate (Publishing Services): Nearly all our work is for established customers at established rates. When we do negotiate on price, it's usually possible to get a good sense of budget constraints and to cut our cloth accordingly.

Paolo (Illustrator/Fine Artist): If the project is large and the client may use me again, some discounts are given. Otherwise, I take into account how much time I will have to spend in preparation or travelling and consider whether the client is a 'fusspot' (this *always* means a lot of extra work).

Leslie (Production Services): Most companies I deal with have set rates. Otherwise I quote recommended union rates and negotiate from there.

Richard (Photographer): The size of the company or magazine circulation. What is the available budget?

Mary (Production Editor): Clients may ask what my rate is for a particular job, but more often they tell me what their rates are. I might accept a lower rate from a client I particularly wanted to work for.

Woodie (Drummer/Programmer): No fees I've received for drumming have been negotiable.

Philip (Advertising/Direct Mail): I negotiate based on whether I think it's easy work and what I think the market will stand.

WHAT WILL YOU ACCEPT?

If you are asking for £20 per hour you may actually be quite willing to accept £15. Deciding this *before* you discuss it with the client means you won't have to make calculations in your head while you are trying to concentrate on the negotiation.

Equally important, if you already know what your limit is, you won't be persuaded to lower it in the heat of the moment.

WHAT DO YOU WANT?

You won't always be negotiating for money alone. Other factors may be just as important, depending on the situation:

- How flexible is the deadline? Will the job fit in with your other commitments? You may negotiate a substantial fee for an urgent piece of work but what

if your regular work suffers as a result? You could jeopardize a steady flow of money in favour of one big pay-off.
- How much autonomy will you have? Can you create the opportunity to make better use of your professional skills or judgement? Could it be a way of establishing a track record doing more involved (and eventually better paid) work than at present?

Consciously or unconsciously you will develop your own set of priorities, based not only on what you want to earn but what you want to achieve.

As we have stressed, your work should reflect a balance between what pays regularly or on time and what creates new opportunities. That way your business can survive and develop.

How ambitious can you be?
The textbook approach to negotiation says 'never accept the first offer'. However, sticking too rigidly to this can be a sure way of antagonizing or alienating prospective clients.

If a client makes you a perfectly acceptable offer it is pointless making a big show of turning it down just because it is their *first* offer.

DO YOU NEED TIME TO THINK?
If a prospective client contacts you, you don't have to give a definite answer straight away. You can always say: 'I'm sure I would be interested, but I'll have to check my other commitments and get back to you.'

They will usually wait to hear from you before trying someone else. This gives you a breathing space to think or get advice before you commit yourself.

OTHER FACTORS
Particularly with more substantial pieces of work, you must find out what you would be committing yourself

to. Establish not only your role, but also the client's responsibilities:

- What specifically you are expected to do and *how* do they want it done?
- Who else is involved and what aspects of the job will *they* be responsible for?
- Will they take responsibility for getting the work to you or letting you get started on time?
- If the work falls behind schedule before you are involved, are you still expected to meet the original deadline?

Once you feel you understand what is involved summarize it in your own words and repeat it back to them: 'Presumably, what this will mean is . . .' This will show them that you understand what they want and also give you the opportunity to clarify what has been said.

ANY COMMON GROUND?

You won't reach agreement unless your objectives are reasonably compatible. If you know that you won't settle for less than £600, and discover that the client won't pay more than £500, there's no point in going any further.

TRADING

Baldly stating 'I must have 50% of the fee in advance' is a bit of an ultimatum. Likewise, making an unprompted offer 'I can easily do it by the end of the month' may only encourage the client to make greater demands.

Linking the two is altogether more constructive:

> 'If you were able to pay 50% of the fee in advance, I could certainly make it a priority and try to have it ready by the end of the month.'

Note: Don't be intimidated into blurting out further concessions if your original offer is met with silence. Allow the client time to think and let them return with either an agreement or a counter-offer.

KNOWING WHEN TO STOP
Everybody has a problem knowing when to stop negotiating. You are under two opposing pressures:

- If you stop too soon you might miss out on a better offer.
- If you carry on you might end up giving more away.

Stop when you feel you have achieved what you wanted. If the client comes back with a counter-offer later on, you may still have some bargaining power in reserve.

Confirming the agreement
Having come to some sort of agreement it is good practice to send a letter confirming it:

> 'Further to our conversation on Thursday (16 June) I look forward to going ahead with the work for the agreed fee of £XXX . . . '

This will pre-empt any disagreement over terms at a later stage.

CHECKLIST
- Not every discussion with a client is a negotiation.
- Negotiate when the situation is open-ended.
- Decide what you are willing to accept in advance.
- Negotiate deadlines and conditions as well as money.
- As ever, balance work that pays regularly and work that creates new opportunities.

- Don't stick too rigidly to rules; sometimes you *can* accept the first offer.
- You don't have to commit yourself straight away.
- Find out exactly what the client wants.
- Can you find any common ground? If not, there's no point going any further.
- Link something you want with something you can offer.
- If your terms are met with silence, don't be intimidated into making further concessions.
- Stop negotiating when you have achieved what you wanted.
- Confirm what has been agreed.

10
GIVE ME THE MONEY!

Invoicing is arguably the most important part of your work. Of course, you hope to enjoy or derive satisfaction from what you do, but you are doing it to get paid.

When you finish a piece of work and put in your invoice it is tempting to regard it as money in the bank. In fact, by the time you have done this, and somebody has bothered to pay you, there will probably be at least two months between actually doing the work and getting any money for it.

HOW TO INVOICE
Your invoice should be clear and informative. It should be easy for the client to see who they are paying and what they are paying for.

Your invoice may be the only written record the client keeps about you, long after they've lost your other details. Make sure it fits in with the image that you put across with other self-promotional material (letter headings, business cards etc).

WHAT TO INCLUDE
Whatever form your invoice takes the following details should be included:

- **Date** – preferably as soon as you have finished the work.
- **Invoice number** – start at a high number so it doesn't look as though you only have a few clients, or don't have much experience.
- **Description of the job** – what you did, along with a relevant job number, if supplied.

- **Who commissioned you** – if it is a large organization, any queries can go straight to your contact, thus saving time.
- **The basis of your charges** – 'X hours at *agreed* rate of £XX per hour', plus expenses if appropriate.
- **The terms of payment** – usually within 30 days.
- **Who cheques should be made payable to** – make sure they spell your name correctly, so there are no delays at the bank.

The clearer and more complete the information you provide, the easier it is for them to process your invoice.

WHEN TO INVOICE

Unless you want to stagger payments for tax purposes, invoice as soon as possible. This means that:

- Your invoice will reach the client before they've had a chance to forget how grateful they were for your efforts.
- What you are owed will still be fresh in your mind and the client's.

Creating a flow

Try to negotiate payment in instalments for work that will last any longer than three weeks. Rather than waiting for a large lump sum at the end of the job, you can then invoice every week. There are several advantages to this:

- Your client won't receive one massive bill but a series of smaller ones. As well as giving the impression of better value for money, the client has more incentive to pay you because they still need you.
- Your cash flow will be healthier. Otherwise, if a job takes two months, and you don't get paid for 30 days, you will be waiting at least three months for your money.

- If the accounts department go on holiday or their computer shuts down (or, even worse, the firm goes out of business) at least part of your account will already have been paid.
- In many organizations, the higher the amount of a cheque, the longer it takes to process because more people may have to sign it. Smaller cheques mean you may well get your money sooner.

LITTLE AND LARGE

It is a commonly held belief that large organizations will keep suppliers (you, for instance) waiting as long as possible for payment. Although this is often true, dealing with larger companies can give you certain safeguards:

- **Bureaucracy** – you can expect proper records to be kept of what was agreed and what is to be paid, and your payment is likely to be handled by competent accounts staff.
- **Hierarchy** – if your client within the company queries the payment you have recourse to people higher up in the chain.

The smaller the client, the less protected you are by established codes of dealing. The money is likely to be coming more directly out of the client's pocket. After the work has been done, and they no longer need you, clients have less incentive to pay up promptly.

If you're approached by a sole trader or other small concern, try to negotiate some advance or interim payments as a show of good faith on their part.

Note: If you have doubts about your client it may be worth checking their status with a credit checking agency.

PROMISES, PROMISES...

It is not uncommon to be promised more and better work in return for patience over payment. Realistically, all this usually means is accumulating a few more unpaid debts, then being passed over in favour of a fresh 'victim'.

This approach may apply equally in negotiations over your fee. The following stories highlight the pitfalls.

David (Press/PR): I once worked on a rather glossy magazine, peddling sports cars and conservatories to 'high fliers'. It was actually run from above an off-licence in a shabby south London suburb and ludicrously underfunded.

The publisher was, however, extremely resourceful. Approaching a new printer each issue he explained how the magazine was not only expanding but likely to come out more frequently. Excited at the prospect of such regular work, each printer would offer a bargain price. Come next issue, of course, the publisher was knocking on a new door . . .

Ian (Graphic Designer): A client complained to me that his printer had told him that I had 'cut corners' on some work. I had actually done as much as I could within the budget, it just meant the printer had to do more preparation. Of course, the printer didn't like that because *he* was being badly paid as well!

I learned *never* to take on work when the client says 'I can't afford to pay much now, but there should be plenty of work in the future.'

CHASING PAYMENTS

Most of us are embarrassed about complaining or making a fuss. It is a common irony that when we are unhappy with something we will talk about it to *anyone* but the person responsible.

Business demands a rather more straightforward approach, and helpfully makes the complaint less of a personal issue. Once an invoice becomes overdue it is perfectly legitimate to contact the client immediately. This can mean little more than having to restate your terms of payment, as detailed on your invoice.

> 'I'm ringing to enquire about my invoice dated XXX for £XXX. As I've already been waiting over a month I thought I'd better make sure it's not lost in the system. Please could you check for me?'

If you are speaking to the client themselves you can afford to get to the point fairly quickly, as they know the details.

On the other hand, if you are dealing with a separate administrator or accounts department always try to be as patient and pleasant as possible. The person you are speaking to will probably be dealing with several calls like yours; having to sort out problems caused by other people.

Take their name and come back to them if necessary: '. . . you were looking into . . . have you had any luck with . . . ? Is there someone else I should check this with?'

RECOVERING YOUR MONEY

If you have no luck politely chasing up your money, what next?

The first thing to consider is whether it's worth it. The time and trouble you take could end up costing you more than the amount of the debt. This is sad and unjust, but nevertheless true.

Where your relationship with a client has broken down to the extent that they refuse to cooperate in paying your monies owed, you may consider the following:

- Get a solicitor to write a letter for you. Like accountants, many solicitors will see you for a free first appointment and give you an estimate of charges. An official letter often persuades clients to pay up.
- Go in person to the client's office. If other customers are there the client may be embarrassed enough to pay you off.

COURT ACTION

If, after all this, you decide that you want to take full legal action, any county court or solicitor will tell you how to proceed.

In theory

This involves applying to the court for the appropriate form and completing it with details of your claim. A summons will then be sent to the defendant (the client). You will have to pay to do this, but you can add the court costs to the debt which you are asking the client to pay.

The defendant is then obliged to pay within 14 days. If not then you (the plaintiff) may have judgement in your favour, which could mean the defendant getting a visit from the bailiffs.

In practice

The sight of a summons, which will be on the client's desk very quickly, can work miracles. Nobody, especially if they are in financial difficulties, wants the adverse publicity of a court case.

PJ: After several weeks of chasing up a payment, the company's vague promises turned to 'we are not making any payments at present'.

I threatened court action and a director promised that if I waited they would pay me when they could. Having already waited three months I explained that if I wasn't paid by return the company would be getting a summons. It was only when the summons actually arrived that they paid up (immediately); not just the original debt, but my costs and expenses as well.

Going through the courts can, however, be time-consuming and expensive. In fact, the threat of legal action is often rather more useful than the process itself.

Liz (Researcher): I have used the county court. It was a very painful experience. A man still didn't pay up after judgement in my favour. Eventually I got about 50% and gave up. I subsequently discovered an acquaintance of mine had got paid in full by literally sitting outside his office with a small baby and telling all his callers that he owed her £250!

GETTING PAID

What the freelancers say

Ian (Graphic Designer): The time can vary between cash on delivery and six months. Generally I receive payment four or five weeks from invoicing – in fact my terms are 30 days. Slow payers get the normal phone calls, starting politely then rapidly deteriorating to include the odd swear word.

Mike & Kate (Publishing Services): Instantly, in some cases! Generally; the bigger, the slower (and maybe, the surer).

Simon (Actor/Voice Coach): Most people pay up eventually, though sometimes you have to make a lot of persuasive phone calls: 'Look mate, I'm just a one-man band struggling to survive. I can't afford to write this off, OK?'

Philip (Advertising/Direct Mail): Average 45 days, chasing is done by phone and fax.

Paolo (Illustrator/Fine Artist): The longest so far is 20 months and still counting. Most pay within a month, fine art sales (at exhibitions) are on the same day.

Leslie (Production Services): Payment has been anything between one week and two and a half months. One new client explained that invoices would only be paid at the end of the month *after* the month in which the invoice was received. I have noticed one or two other companies trying to adopt this approach to delay payment.

Richard (Photographer): Late payers are subjected to frequent telephone calls!

Liz (Researcher): The bigger the firm, the slower the payments – but on the whole I think this is less of a problem now.

Anne (Counsellor): With the courses I run, people pay deposits in advance and I collect the rest on the day. With counselling I'm paid at the end of *every* session.

Nancy (Writer/Editor): I am generally paid within three to six weeks, but have had to ask for help from the NUJ on one or two occasions.

CHECKLIST

- However much you enjoy your work, you *are* doing it to earn a living.
- Invoicing and chasing payments are essential to your survival as a freelancer.
- Make invoices clear and informative, and in line with your image.
- Always include certain basic details: date, number, description, contact, charges, payment terms, payee.
- Send your invoice as soon as possible.
- Negotiate payment in instalments for long jobs.
- Large, established companies give you some safeguards of payment.
- Patience is not always rewarded.
- Contact your client as soon as the money becomes overdue.
- Recover bad debts by: solicitor's letter, personal visit or court action.

11
WORKING FROM HOME

Having said 'Cheerio' to your full-time routine, will your daily activities have lost their structure? Not surprisingly we often tend to associate rules or timetables with an attack on our freedom: 'Keep off the grass . . . no parking . . . tidy your room . . . lights out at eight o'clock.'

When you become your own boss, however, they provide you with a useful framework on which to build. It is by doing the things that we have to that we can do the things we want to.

HOMESPUN PHILOSOPHY
The following points are a combination of accepted theory and practical tips from which you can develop your own ideas.

Get up at a regular time
If you don't, you may fall into the habit of getting up later and later. Linking this in with something you have to do each day makes it a lot easier. This is one occasion when a regular household chore or errand can be a help (for instance giving your 'other half' a lift to work, making breakfast, collecting the papers etc).

Get dressed!
You don't want to feel a mess: dress comfortably but be presentable. This includes wearing more formal or businesslike clothes if they are what you feel most comfortable in. Without their uniform some people, even on the telephone, feel at a disadvantage.

Organize a proper office area for yourself
Where you are working in a family home or shared accommodation this makes it clear to those around you

that although you are in during the day you are nevertheless working. You are *not* available for daytime errands (shopping, housework etc) any more than they are.

Leslie (Production Services): My children found it hard to understand that I was working when I was at home. Eventually, I realized that I would need a purpose-built office and had an extension built. Now my problem is getting out and closing the door on my work.

Have what you need close at hand and avoid cluttering the area up with too many non-essentials. It should be a haven from half-finished ironing, dirty washing or anything you may be tempted to attend to as an alternative to your work. Making it into a den, crammed full of your favourite knick-knacks, can be more of a distraction than an inspiration.

Try to be tidy

Although you are not expecting to be featured in *Homes and Gardens* you do need to know where things are. Hunting for a stapler or other essential piece of equipment will waste time and destroy the flow of your work.

Keeping your work in order also means that if a client rings you with a query you are less likely to leave them hanging on the line while you rummage through a stack of papers a foot high.

(Nevertheless, both halves of this writing partnership are far from obsessive about tidiness. Do whatever helps you get the job done, but don't spend more time colour coding your files than you do on the actual work.)

Make routine calls in batches

This could apply to things like invoice chasing or other administration. Rather than hanging around waiting

WORKING FROM HOME

for someone to get off the phone, or come out of their meeting, you can merely try the next on your list.

Avoid rambling personal calls
Of course it's one thing getting away with it while you're a full-time employee, but quite another when you notch up long, peak rate calls in your own time. These calls:

- waste time in the working day that you will have to make up later on;
- tie up the line so clients can't get through;
- perpetuate the image that you are not working.

Unplug the television
Unfortunately, for those of us who miss the social aspects of a full-time environment, a bit of harmless television during a tea break seems to fill the void. Half an hour later, you'll still be sitting there unable to resist another feature 'coming up after the break'.

Only use one mug
No sniggering at the back, this really does work. You will keep one mug clean as you go along, rather than having your entire collection of them dotted around the place with half an inch of cold tea or coffee congealing in the bottom. (Even better, buy yourself a thermos flask, which saves endlessly boiling kettles.)

Having breaks
No one can work non-stop for ever. After a while you will tire and lose concentration and your pace of work will get slower.

A short break away from your desk every 35–40 minutes will circulate oxygen to the brain and keep your mind sharp. Pacing yourself in this way will help you achieve more in a day and be less tired at the end of it.

Go out for a while every day
Some work projects seem to become all-consuming. Without those helpful nine-to-five boundaries things get a little blurred around the edges and it is very easy to isolate yourself. No matter how busy you are, going out, even for a short while, helps refresh you and restore a sense of perspective.

Eat regularly and sensibly
Working on your own it can be an effort to prepare real food. It's easy to treat the day as one long tea break, snacking on crisps and biscuits; or forgetting to eat at all. One way around this is to go out to lunch in a cafe, or buy sandwiches like you would if you were in an employer's office. (Fresh fruit is an excellent substitute for sweets and snacks.)

Learn to switch off
Once you have decided to stop, shut the door on your work and do something else. This is another reason for trying to keep your office environment and home environment separate.

Exercise
This can serve three useful purposes: first, it is a way of keeping healthy (remember, no more sick leave); second, regular exercise helps form part of routine; third, if it is at a local gym or by way of classes, it provides social contact. You also have the option of using local facilities at off-peak times.

Give yourself something to look forward to
'If I can stick at this till 5 o'clock, I can relax this evening.' This is another way to help define the boundaries of your work.

TAKING TIME OFF
Apparently, freelancers are not supposed to have holidays, weekends or evenings off.

In our experience, most clients assume evenings and weekends are all part of the service. Only on rare occasions has anyone offered overtime rates or considered that we may not be available at these times.

Giving clients notice you are going to be away on holiday often results in them not contacting you for a couple of months: 'We weren't sure when you were coming back.' (Always ring them just to let them know you *are* back.)

Diminishing returns

This implied pressure conspires to widen the boundaries of your work to a point at which it becomes all-encompassing. Many freelancers even find it difficult to take time off during slack periods as they feel that all their energies should be devoted to finding the next piece of work.

However, by succumbing to these pressures you will become stale and fatigued; spending more time achieving less.

You might find it impossible to relax at home; phone calls and letters keep coming and wherever you look there's a reminder of what you should be doing. If so, it is in the best interests of your work that you get out and take a proper break.

ISOLATION

Will you miss being around people? The chances are you will. Depending on the nature of your work, you may find yourself hardly speaking to anybody from one day to the next. You may equally find that you have nobody to talk to about anything but work. This makes it difficult to switch off and recharge your batteries.

For gregarious types the effects are obvious; no more

chatting around the photocopier or drinks machines, and no more office parties for that matter!

For the less outgoing the effects are more subtle. Without the imposed interaction it is very easy to retreat even further. This can lead to a massive lack of confidence when it comes to dealing with people.

- If opportunities to work on-site/in-house arise do take them. If you haven't had to work with a client looking over your shoulder you may feel apprehensive (disinclined to break up your cosy home working routine) but avoiding it merely makes you more isolated.
- Without wittering on, and wasting the client's time, try to develop some rapport over the telephone. Even if this initially only extends as far as finding out how the last work you were involved in has turned out, it helps both of you to feel that you are part of a team.

DISTRACTIONS

Working from home leaves you vulnerable to a number of new distractions and interruptions.

Other people's attitudes (family and friends)

As we have seen before, it is important to make people aware that although you are at home you are working. Getting this message across can be something of an uphill struggle; if you're there, what's to stop you from hanging out the washing or going to the shops?

It is therefore important to emphasize the effect that these interruptions have on your concentration or productivity, although they may appear minor in isolation. The onus is on you to adopt a recognizably professional approach. If you appear to take days off arbitrarily or always seem to be watching television when they ring you, they will not take your work seriously.

You *are* at work. Whatever limitations on errands or personal calls would have applied at your last full-time job should still, by implication, apply now. You may feel that this strict approach is at odds with the flexibility and freedom that freelancing should represent. In fact, the opposite is true. Defining these boundaries allows you to concentrate on what *you* want to do.

Remember: Nobody can see when you're thinking:

One successful author noted how his mother-in-law would stride into his office while he was pacing about plotting his next novel and say: 'As you're not doing anything you can give me a lift to the shops.'

A plague of meter readers

Public utilities, such as gas and electricity, bring with them maintenance engineers and meter readers. These apparently have no idea where they will be from one day to the next.

Your time is valuable. You do not want important telephone calls or meetings interrupted by the gas man arriving three hours late. Pinning them down to a reasonably specific time, which you are entitled to do, just gives you one less thing to worry about or be distracted by.

Leisure pursuits

Remember that it is these distractions which interrupt your work, not the other way around.

> 'The trouble with doing nothing is that you can never take any time off.'
>
> *Hoagy Carmichael*

Other work

Variety is one of the great benefits of freelancing. Becoming bogged down on one piece of work *can* be alleviated by passing on to another. (Mundane, mechanical work, for instance, can free the more creative parts of the mind, when you feel you have run out of ideas.)

On the other hand, don't dodge awkward issues; although some things improve with a fresh perspective, others must be faced head on. (If you know a deadline is going to slip or an idea just isn't going to work, going away and coming back to it merely leaves less time to deal with the consequences.)

DISTRACTIONS

What the freelancers say

Simon (Actor/Voice Coach): Endless phone calls, social visitors etc. There's always a conflict between domestic and professional demands upon one's time.

Ian (Graphic Designer): Usually friends ringing up, but I've learnt to put them off.

Liz (Researcher): The front door bell! In younger days, it was being asked to look after other people's children. You must learn to say 'No' and be firm.

Woodie (Drummer/Programmer): I worked from home for two years on a studio-based project. Dividing my social life and music was hard as music was always connected with my friends.

Philip (Advertising/Direct Mail): The proximity of my leisure pursuits.

Anne (Counsellor): Gardening and housework, keeping everything neat and in order rather than dealing with major pieces of work.

Richard (Photographer): Television and losing concentration as I'm sidetracked into things not associated with work.

Nancy (Writer/Editor): My son (almost 12 years old) when he's home from school.

Paolo (Illustrator/Fine Artist): My baby daughter! Also clients phoning me half way through their projects to change things.

CHECKLIST
- Try to get up at the same time every day.
- Organize a proper office area.
- Make routine phone calls in batches.
- Avoid personal calls during working hours.
- Make sure you have breaks and go out at least once a day.
- Define boundaries for your work so it doesn't become all-consuming.
- Counteract isolation by working in-house occasionally.
- Adopt a recognizable professional approach to keep family and friends aware that you *are* working.
- Value your own time.

12
LIFELINES

Far from being the looming monsters they sometimes appear, deadlines can be helpful lifelines. Instead of wasting time deciding what to do first, your prioritizing is often done for you. Deadlines help to restore some of the structure of your old routine.

> 'Do we not all find freedom to improvise, in all art, in all life, along the guiding lines of discipline?'
> *Yehudi Menuhin*

Precisely because freelancing offers so much flexibility, two of the most difficult things are:

- getting started on work; and
- knowing when to stop.

GETTING GOING
Many of us are capable of sustained periods of great productivity but have enormous difficulties in actually getting under way.

In our experience, the more flexible the deadline the more difficult it is to get started and the longer things take. Working on more involved or inspiring projects, or being offered more responsibility, can compound this effect:

1. **Elation** – It's just the chance you've been looking for to show what you can really do; safe, for the moment, from the reality of what it might entail. (Mentally, you've probably already spent the money and are rehearsing a self-deprecating reference to your success for the next social function.)
2. **Prevarication** – You really should have got started

by now, but the deadline is probably far enough away to actively *encourage* you to hesitate. After all, you want to get this right, don't you? You have so many good ideas you don't know where to begin.
3. **Panic** – In the cold light of day your ideas add up to an approach that needs more work than you had thought. You realize that you have spent half your available time stalling and daydreaming. The deadline looms large and you find yourself rushing and cutting corners to get finished on time.

This is hardly the end result you would have expected or wanted. All that was needed was some realistic forward planning.

STEPPING STONES
Instead of relying on one overall deadline provided by the client, you need to map out your own series of intermediate deadlines; in other words draw up some kind of schedule. This will allow you to work out what proportion of the time can be devoted to each phase.

If you find your own deadlines slipping it is a valuable early warning that the overall project is in danger of falling behind. It is better to be strict with yourself and leave a margin for error. Work on the basis that the *next* stage is always going to take a bit longer than you think.

SCHEDULING
Overall, you need to keep track of your flow of work. This should go some way to pre-empting either overloading or large gaps between jobs.

Leslie (Production Services): I draw up a spreadsheet two months ahead, which shows me what work there is and allows me to see where other work can be fitted in. I always log how long a piece of work takes, even if it is not paid by the hour. I can then work out how long a similar commission will take next time and quote or plan accordingly.

PERFECT FREELANCING

What none of this can take into account are the vagaries of clients' timetables.

Mary (Production Editor): When I have problems taking on too much work, it is usually by assuming that each job will come along and be completed in order. I quite often experience log-jams of work because clients' schedules and deadlines have slipped.

This also highlights the need to establish what happens to *your* deadlines when the client falls behind.

PRIORITIZING

Try to establish some kind of criteria for prioritizing your work. You can then make choices *before* you become overloaded. The following are a variety of approaches which may give you a guide:

- Are some deadlines more flexible than others?
- Are there regular clients who should take precedence? Can you fit other work around them?
- Which work is actually needed first?
- Is there anything that you can get out of the way quickly?
- Is any of the work particularly lucrative, or likely to lead to something better?

Not all of these appear compatible, but a great deal depends on the circumstances. As we continually emphasize, you should be looking to find a balance between giving priority to work which pays regularly and work which creates new opportunities for you.

The average freelancer will probably mix and match these to suit:

Ian (Graphic Designer): I try to deal with work as it arrives. Beyond that, all jobs are equal, from minimum rate work to extremely well-paid projects.

Simon (Actor/Voice Coach): I try and deal with everything as soon as it comes up; giving priority to the most creatively fulfilling opportunities.

Paolo (Illustrator/Fine Artist): By deadlines. Any urgent requests come first along with best clients.

Leslie (Production Services): As I have a number of regular clients, I tend to fit other work around these. Obviously, the regular work takes priority.

Richard (Photographer): Is there a lot of travelling or aggravation involved? Who will pay up quickly or generously?

Philip (Advertising/Direct Mail): Either in order of deadline or by getting the easy victories out of the way first.

PRIORITIZING THROUGH PRESSURE

When everything has come at once, you need to have a way of jettisoning any non-essential elements. A recognized way of doing this is to create lists under the following headings:

- What *must* be done.
- What *should* be done.
- What you would *like* to get done.

Some freelancers would take 'non-essential elements' to mean eating and sleeping, but going without either is not going to help much.

There are, however, a number of things you can do:

- Consider delegating. There may be simple, mechanical aspects of your work that could be taken over by someone else relatively cheaply, while you concentrate on important jobs.
- See if any meetings can be postponed or replaced with brief telephone calls, letters or faxes.
- Put on your answering machine and screen your calls. Only deal with those you absolutely have to.
- Arrange travelling for off-peak time so that you are not held up in traffic.

- Long journeys by train allow you to catch up with work or take a well-earned break (equivalent car journeys generally provide neither).
- Necessary errands such as paying money in at the bank or posting work should be timed to avoid busy periods (lunch hours, for instance).

Note: Even when the immediate rush is over, these re-assessments will help you to have a more sharply defined sense of priorities.

SLACK PERIODS

There will be times when you are up to date with your work and nothing new appears on your freelance horizon. Even if some free time could be a much-needed break, many freelancers find it impossible to relax unless they know where the next job is coming from.

If regular clients don't give you any work for a while, it is easy to assume that they don't want you any more. In reality, there may just not be that much for you to do. By all means give them a ring to find out how things are going, but don't pester them or appear desperate.

We have already stressed the importance of cultivating a number of clients. Even when you progress onto better or more lucrative work, keep a contact with old clients who may still have work for you when you need it.

Note: Freelancers in more precarious or seasonal work often have casual jobs to keep them going during gaps. If you have 'bread and butter' work that you can turn your hand to, so much the better, but don't be sidetracked.

What the freelancers say

Ian (Graphic Designer): There are normally a few things to do that have been shelved for a while. If not, I just use the time to do other things, knowing that there'll come a point when I'm rushed off my feet again.

Anne (Counsellor): During slack periods I just skip off and enjoy myself.

Paolo (Illustrator/Fine Artist): I do my paperwork, deal with my accounts and work on self-promotional projects.

Mike & Kate (Publishing Services): We don't feel demotivated, just *terrified*. A slack period with (a) money in the bank; (b) the guarantee of work at the end of it; now *that's* want we'd like. (And we certainly wouldn't waste it catching up on paperwork.)

Liz (Researcher): I certainly feel demotivated, a bit like an actor who thinks every job is his/her last.

Philip (Advertising/Direct Mail): *Nothing* gets done without a looming deadline as incentive.

Leslie (Production Services): I don't have slack periods . . .

Richard (Photographer): A lot of my work is based around social/sporting events and Royal engagements so I know when slack times will be. Busy times are so hectic it's quite easy to grind to a halt altogether when a gap appears.

Using the gaps constructively

Of all these approaches, we would identify most readily with Ian's view that 'I just use the time to do other things, knowing that there'll come a point when I'm rushed off my feet again.'

For every gap there is likely to be a glut. Your forward planning is merely an attempt to smooth out inevitable peaks and troughs.

If you can break through the psychological barrier of feeling unemployed and fearing for your next pay cheque these gaps can be put to good use:

- updating your promotional material;
- finding new clients;
- trying new markets;

- taking stock (are you achieving what you set out to do?);
- updating your skills.

If you have heavy financial commitments (family, mortgage etc) this may all seem rather impractical. On the other hand, will you be fulfilling your commitments any better by worrying more earnestly, or by settling for a treadmill of inferior jobs that you can't escape?

Rather than fretting over work that may just not be there, all of these allow you to do something constructive about what happens next.

CHECKLIST
- Flexible deadlines make it easier to prevaricate and so you need a more disciplined approach.
- Create deadlines for each stage of a project to keep on schedule.
- Work on the basis that the *next* stage will always take longer than you think.
- Try to establish a way of prioritizing your work.
- Work out what *must* be done, what *should* be done and what you would *like* to get done.
- Consider delegating straightforward tasks if you are overloaded.
- Use slack periods constructively. Don't panic.

13
SAYING 'NO' TO WORK

One of the most difficult things for a freelancer to do is to say 'No' to work. Mindful of eager competitors and unsure of where next month's pay cheque is coming from, you may feel that:

- If you turn away a new client they will never ask you again.
- If you can't accommodate a regular client your existing work will be taken over by whoever fills in and you'll never get it back.

If fact, by taking on work that you are not in a position to do properly you will end up with the same net result . . . lost clients.

ARE YOU OVERWORKED?
- Do you often work after 8pm?
- Do you take work to bed?
- Do you dream about your work?
- Do you often work through the night?
- Do you work at weekends?
- Do you take work on holiday?
- How often do you cancel or avoid social events because you are too busy?
- Can you stop thinking about work when you go out?
- Are you always tired?
- Are you prone to minor ailments, like colds?

EFFECTS OF OVERLOADING
Working long hours at peak times is one thing. Being constantly overloaded with work is quite another. So what happens?

1. **You rush** – As you try to meet the deadline you are

unable to give your work the time it needs. The first thing to suffer (apart from your nerves) is usually quality. Although a certain amount of pressure can be like a shot of adrenalin, too much merely wears you down.

2. **Fatigue sets in** – When you become tired, everything starts taking twice as long. You spend more time sorting out mistakes than making progress. Eventually you become so tired that you cannot work out what is important and what isn't.

3. **Too many irons in the fire** – You try to do several things at once and get confused between them. Jobs get put to one side as more urgent priorities come up. You then go back to the original work and probably end up doing some of it twice, or missing bits, because you forget where you were up to. Everything suffers.

4. **You hide** – You don't want to speak to your clients any more, for fear that they will either pressurize you further or pick up on your obvious panic.

5. **You are overwhelmed** – You have so much work to do that you don't know where to start. You end up running to stand still.

JUST SAY 'NO'

Difficult as it is, there are times when you really should turn down work.

When you're already too busy

Don't risk taking on something you haven't got time to do properly. If you can't delegate then turn it down. Clients will respect the fact that you are obviously in demand and will probably try you again in future. If you take the job and do it badly, they won't call back.

When you don't want to encourage the client

Some clients pay low rates, or are demanding and inconsiderate. Once you've worked for them, and found out the hard way, don't expect them to improve. Keep them at the bottom of your list, just in case, but they are best avoided.

When the client owes you money
If a client never got around to paying you for the last job, don't be tempted to do any more work until they have paid you what they owe. You are working to be paid, not just to keep yourself busy.

When the work is beyond your abilities
We wouldn't suggest turning something down just because it's difficult. Everything new is difficult at first, and if you don't accept challenges you'll never progress.

If, however, you know it's too big a step (perhaps requiring a skill or specialist knowledge you just don't have) it's safer to turn it down than to risk a terrible disaster which could affect your confidence and reputation.

When the work is beyond your capacity
If a project would quite obviously require more than one person's input, don't try to take it on and do everything yourself. Although this could appear a lucrative prospect, there are only so many hours in a day, and only so much one person can do.

When one client takes over
Work which demands all your time for a long period will not be bad news to everybody. Only you can judge. Although working exclusively for one client for several months can give you financial security, and make life generally easier, it also has drawbacks:

- You will have to neglect the other clients you have built up, and risk them finding someone to take your place.

- The Inland Revenue could reclassify you as an employee.
- You can become so dependent on this client that you lose your professional freedom.

When the work could jeopardize your reputation

We are not suggesting you get ideas above your station. Nevertheless, you will probably have put a good deal of effort into building up your clients and establishing your professionalism. Your association with certain projects may undermine this.

If a client is incompetent or intent on cutting corners you could end up being associated with a disaster. No matter how professional *your* contribution may have been, other people will only judge the end result.

When you feel a project is unethical

Is the client using your skills to help them mislead, exploit, oppress or endanger others? Only you can decide what is acceptable to you.

SENDING WORK BACK

Do a client's requirements or deadlines keep changing from what has been agreed? If so, you could find yourself endangering the rest of your schedule while the client gets organized.

When you do have to send work back, be careful to ensure that nothing you have or haven't done can be used by clients to justify *their* poor planning. If you give the impression that you have been unprofessional or arbitrary, you could end up taking responsibility for everything that has gone awry.

Note: Wherever you see a client poised at the top of a long slippery slope, always make sure that, whatever happens, you do *your* part of the job in as thorough and blameless a way as possible.

SAYING 'NO' TO WORK

CHECKLIST
- Turning down work does not mean the client will never ask you again.
- Taking on too much jeopardizes *all* your work.
- Avoid work that you haven't got time to do properly.
- Don't try to do work way beyond your abilities or capacity.
- Certain types of project will reflect badly on you (unethical, shoddy etc).
- Don't encourage clients who are bad payers or bad employers.
- If you take on work you have no feel for, quality will suffer.
- Don't cancel work arbitrarily, but if clients keep missing *their* deadlines consider the effect on the rest of your schedule.

14
IF THINGS GO WRONG

Things *do* go wrong. Sometimes several of them at once. Occasionally *everything* seems to take a nosedive at the same time.

More often than not, we arrive at this last situation by succumbing to the first two . . . and panicking.

This chapter is an attempt to help avoid things getting any worse than they have to. If you can recognize the likely pitfalls you should even be able to pre-empt some of them.

Anyway, as we said, things *do* go wrong . . .

WHAT WENT WRONG?
Two of the greatest failings you can have as a freelancer are:

- never blaming yourself for anything that goes wrong; and
- blaming yourself for everything that goes wrong.

Why am I surrounded by incompetents?
Not being in a big hurry to confess your slip-ups to the client is one thing; starting to believe your own excuses is quite another.

So many situations are open to interpretation that it can be very easy never to accept *any* responsibility.

Say, for instance, you find yourself at odds with the client's approach, and the work suffers. Why did it happen?

- The client didn't know what they were doing.

- The client knew what *they* wanted but you decided that *you* knew better.

Realistically, the second version may not even enter your head, but rather than instinctively shifting responsibility elsewhere it at least gives you the chance to think about what happened. Although you may ultimately arrive back at the first conclusion (it *is* rather tempting), you should still learn something useful for next time.

Is the customer always right?

When a piece of work has not gone that well, it is good practice to look first at what you could or should have done and try to learn from this. Nevertheless, this does not mean that you must automatically take responsibility for everything.

Rosemary (Proofreader): Working in-house a member of the client firm said 'I have checked this work and marked the corrections. Just make sure these are done, I don't want you to waste time checking the whole thing again.'

I felt that in the circumstances it was more professional to do what was asked than to insist on doing a 'proper job' and appear pedantic. By the time the work reached its next stage it still had mistakes in it. The person involved was in no big hurry to acknowledge what he had missed; it looked as if I had not done my job properly.

Frankly, it can be rather too easy for the freelancer to become a 'sacrificial lamb' where things go wrong. The client will be protecting their own long-term interests. If a slip-up will reflect badly on them it is much easier to blame it on someone just passing through . . . that's you, we're afraid.

The only real answer in these situations (other than not

PERFECT FREELANCING

doing the work) is to make a written reference to what you have done 'as specified'.

BEING HONEST WITH YOURSELF

It is only by being honest about where you have gone wrong that you can properly acknowledge what you have done right. Give yourself credit where it is due but don't be so defensive about criticism that you can't learn by your mistakes.

IT HAPPENED!

By no mean exhaustive, these examples give an insight into some of the thornier issues that may arise.

What do you do if you need extra time but know the deadlines are tight?

PJ: Eager to accommodate a new client, I agreed to take on some urgent work. I was already overloaded so I had to rush through it to meet the deadline.

For a long time I heard nothing from the client. I rang her to check that the job had been satisfactory. Of course, it hadn't; it was riddled with inaccuracies and mistakes.

The client would never have told me this had I not rung. She would just have never used me again . . . and, in fact, never did!

Whether it is a new client or an existing one we are all anxious to please (and mindful of competitors ready to undercut us in some way). Nevertheless, there has to be honest communication between you.

Always keep the client informed. What you *should never do* (although it is often done) is leave it until the last minute before you spring the bad news and pretend it is as big a surprise to you as it is to the client.

Don't be too embarrassed to explain the situation. The sooner you inform the client, the sooner you can both find a way round the problem.

What do you do if a client agreed a fee for a specific job, and either offers a lower figure on completion or asks you to do extra work without reference to additional pay?

SM: A new client explained that although he could not pay very much initially, the company was growing and I would soon be paid more.

As time went on, the workload increased and the pay didn't. I told the client that if the money did not improve I would have to leave the project. He seemed sympathetic and said I would be paid £X a day more, starting that week.

Come the next pay day I was paid precisely the same as before; leaving me short a few hundred pounds. Although annoyed, there was nothing I could do, because I had been too polite to ask for written confirmation of the new arrangement.

If you are asked to do work that goes some way beyond an original agreement, there are a couple of issues that you should consider:

- Is it a regular client with whom you have a flexible and mutually cooperative relationship? (There may well be legitimate reasons, but be careful not to set an over-generous precedent. Let's face it, even among family and friends the most worthy of us are quite capable of taking each other for granted.)
- Is it a new client who could be a source of regular and lucrative work? (Well, possibly, but if this their way of working perhaps it may not turn out to be quite so lucrative after all.)

Taking these into account you may decide merely to learn from the experience. However, there are some practical steps you can take if you feel an agreement has been breached:

- If your client has a superior, explain your problem to them. If they agree with you they may influence your client or overrule their decision in your favour.
- Register your unhappiness with this apparent breach of good faith. If this doesn't get a positive response, mention the possibility of legal action. (This is dealt with in more detail in Appendix A 'Tax & Legal'.)

You feel that a client's requirements fail to take technical practicalities or likely end results into account

A designer produced a glossy brochure for a coach company. Photographs of the fleet had been taken and a picture of a smart young courier was to appear on the cover.

The client, who owned the company, enthusiastically explained that he wanted the face of the courier replaced with that of his beloved wife. Given that the courier was some 30 years younger and rather trimmer, the end result would have been distinctly surreal and rather unflattering.

The designer applauded his client's inventiveness, but carefully pointed out that marrying up the images, for 'technical reasons', could be rather tricky.

At some point or another we may well all be tempted to laugh up our sleeves at a client's naive ideas or failure to grasp the practicalities of our work.

> 'An ignoramus is someone who doesn't know something you learned yesterday.'
>
> *Anon*

IF THINGS GO WRONG

The client *is* employing you for your technical expertise. Often your job entails translating their unrealistic requirements into a workable approach.

You should query the client's instructions tactfully. Remember it is generally better to use a question 'Do you think that . . . ?' than a bald statement 'If you do that it won't work.'

By virtue of a good working relationship with a client who represents a large company you have come to rely on them as a source of regular work. What do you do if they are replaced?

SM: I'd come to rely on one particular client for a steady flow of work. He always seemed to have plenty for me to do. This meant that for long stretches I didn't have to think about where the next job might be coming from.

Unfortunately, particularly for him, he was made redundant and was not going to be replaced. I suddenly found myself with no work. I had neglected other clients for some time and now had nothing to fall back on.

The turnover of full-time staff being what it is nowadays, we would again advise a varied portfolio of clients. Should a 'new broom' replace one of your old friends, a regular source of income could disappear overnight.

It is of course possible that your old client will find work in a similar field and call upon your services again; remember to keep in touch.

As to the original company, you must obviously establish who your contact's successor is (if there is one) and introduce yourself. The chances are they will be glad to hear from a freelancer already familiar with company practices. You could be less of a risk to their credibility than bringing in someone new; particularly if you have a proven track record with the company.

CHECKLIST
- Be honest with yourself about what went wrong.
- Give yourself credit where due but don't be defensive about learning from your own mistakes.
- Face serious issues, if you dodge them they will just get worse.
- Get financial agreements or client specifications in writing where possible.
- Guide clients but don't bully them or ridicule them.
- Keep a varied portfolio of clients; don't put all your eggs in one basket.
- Don't panic. Step back from problems to see what can be salvaged.

Appendix A
TAX & LEGAL

As you are not reading four volumes of *Practical Bookkeeping* we can't tell you everything you need to know about your accounts here. What we aim to do instead is give you some general information on what's involved and help you understand the basic principles.

DO YOU NEED AN ACCOUNTANT?

If your turnover (the total amount you earn) is below £15,000 for the year the Inland Revenue will only require simplified accounts. These consist of:

Turnover (or Sales) − Expenses = Profit

There's no reason why you can't do this for yourself, particularly if you are a methodical person who keeps accurate records. You can also deal with the tax office yourself. They provide instructions for preparing your own accounts and will explain them to you if you ask.

The key phrase here is 'a methodical person who keeps accurate records'. In among all the other new responsibilities you have, can you sustain this approach beyond your initial good intentions?

Would the time that you spend preparing your accounts be better spent on running your business?

What can an accountant offer you? He or she can:

- give advice on what books and records you need to keep;
- be on professional terms with the tax office, check your income tax assessments and appeal against over-assessments;

- advise you on which expenses are tax deductible and how to present them;
- keep up to date with changes in financial law and practice;
- help you approach the bank if you need money to expand;
- advise you on when and whether to form a company and what your obligations are if you do.

In addition, accountants' fees are tax deductible. Hurrah!

CHOOSING AN ACCOUNTANT

If you know other freelancers in a similar position to yourself, the simplest way is to ask them who they recommend.

Otherwise, choosing an accountant can end up being about as scientific as going through the *Yellow Pages*, ringing a few, and picking out the cheapest or most helpful.

The next step is to have a meeting with any 'hopefuls', which should be free of charge (but do check this first). This is an opportunity to ask a few relevant questions.

What kind of clients do they generally deal with?

Asking this before they have any details about your own business may elicit a more revealing answer.

If they are used to dealing with high turnovers and large corporate clients your relatively insignificant custom is not likely to command much priority. You could end up paying over the odds, merely to have your accounts dealt with by a junior member of staff.

Try to find someone who already caters for clients like yourself, as they should understand your needs.

TAX & LEGAL

What will they do, for how much?
If they are evasive about what they will do or refuse to quote a likely figure this may spell trouble. There are many accountants who will offer you a free first consultation where they will give you an estimate, and it makes sense to go to these.

It is always worth getting more than one estimate, but do not base your choice on money alone, find somebody you feel you can trust.

Remember that your accountant will base charges on the amount of time they think they will have to spend on your records. Do your best to appear well organized.

INCOME TAX
In our experience, the Inland Revenue are only too happy to help. A mixture of fear and prejudice often discourages people from contacting them. In fact, they will be as interested as you are in getting things right.

Using the tax system
It is important to remember that although your tax situation will be more complicated when you are self-employed, you will benefit in the end:

- You will pay *less* tax than an employee (you are only taxed on your profit, not on all your earnings).
- You will pay the tax *later* than an employee would. Someone on PAYE has tax deducted before they are paid, you may well have the money in hand for several months before tax is due.

In the beginning
When you start working for yourself it is your responsibility to contact the tax office and let them know of your situation. If you do not do so, they will catch up

with you and you may end up paying much more than you need to.

What will happen next?
Once your accounts have been submitted and agreed to you will be sent an assessment. This will show your income, your allowances (the amount you can earn before tax), how much tax is due and how it has been worked out. You will have to pay this tax in two instalments, in July and January.

Always check your assessment carefully and ask the tax office about anything you don't understand.

SELF-EMPLOYED OR EMPLOYEE?
If the Inland Revenue accepts that you are self-employed you pay tax under what is known as Schedule D. (People classed as employees pay under Schedule E.)

The Revenue prefer to classify people as employees, because they can claim more tax this way. You must be ready to prove you are self-employed.

Proving you are self-employed
This largely depends on how much control you have over the way your job is done. You are likely to be seen as self-employed if:

- you choose how, where and when you do a job;
- you have several clients rather than only one or two;
- you provide your own equipment and materials.

KEEPING RECORDS
Whoever prepares your accounts, you need to keep records of your income and expenses. The more information you can provide, the more easily and quickly you (or your accountant) can extract the necessary details.

TAX & LEGAL

Some documents, like bank statements, can be replaced if you have lost them, but they still have to be paid for.

If you don't provide accounts, the Revenue will estimate how much you owe them (probably more than you actually do).

YOUR INCOME
Recording your income is very simple. Keep a copy of your invoices in date order. Keep a copy of your paying-in books and bank and building society statements to show when money was received.

At the end of your year of trading you, or your accountant, can add up your earnings. This will form the 'turnover' figure on your annual accounts.

YOUR EXPENSES
You must be able to prove what you have spent. You do this by keeping receipts, bills, cheque books and records of cash expenditure.

We would suggest using a file each for your major bills (telephone, car expenses etc). If that seems too complicated use a spike or a cardboard box just for business expenses which you, or your accountant, can sort out at the end of the year.

Allowable business expenses
Expenses which arise *only* from you carrying out your trade or profession can be deducted from your income before it is taxed.

Examples of allowable expenses include:

- office expenses (or a proportion of your rent/mortgage if you work from home);
- stationery and office supplies;

- materials used for the business;
- telephone, electricity and gas for business use;
- travel for business purposes;
- interest on business loans;
- insurance for business purposes.

Setting off expenses
Where items are used for both business and private use, the proportion of each has to be worked out. (The reason for this is that you can only set off the business part of the expense against tax.)

The idea is to claim a reasonable proportion and have evidence to back this up.

CAPITAL ALLOWANCE
Any items with a long-term value (motor vehicles, machinery, specialist equipment etc) are classed as capital expenditure and need different accounting treatment. (See your accountant or tax office about this.)

PENSIONS
You do not *have* to provide for your own pension. However you can get tax relief on personal pension contributions, the rate of relief gets higher as you get older.

INSURANCE
You can't rely on a domestic policy to insure your business assets. Contact an insurance broker who will find a policy which suits your needs.

NATIONAL INSURANCE
Like taxation, you have a legal obligation to pay whichever one(s) apply to you. You can be prosecuted if you don't. However, they are not tax deductible.

LOSSES
Losses can be a good thing from a tax point of view. In some cases you can set off a loss against other income to reduce the amount of tax you pay.

CAPITAL GAINS TAX
If you make a profit on the sale of your house, and have claimed mortgage costs against tax, you may find yourself liable to capital gains tax (CGT) on a proportion of this profit.

VAT
If your turnover is above a certain level (in the region of £45,000 or more per year) you must register for VAT. If your earnings are below the threshold you can still register voluntarily.

The main advantage of registration is that you can claim back the VAT you pay on business purchases.

The disadvantages are:

- You will have to charge VAT on the goods and services you provide and therefore will have to charge clients more.
- You have to keep detailed records and send in returns every three months.
- VAT inspectors can examine your books at any time.

IS IT LEGAL TO WORK FROM HOME?
Whether you rent or own there may be obstacles in the way of your operating a business from home. These are designed to stop people operating scrapyards and noisy factories which could bring down the property value.

If you are not causing a nuisance or lowering the property value it is unlikely anybody will want to stop you working at home.

Appendix B
CONTACTS

ARELS-FELCO (Association of Recognised English Language Schools – Federation of English Language Course Organisations)
2 Pontypool Place, Valentine Place, London SE1 8QF
Tel: 0171 242 3136
Members teach English as foreign language.

Association of British Investigators
ABI House, 10 Bonner Hill Road, Kingston upon Thames, Surrey KT1 3EP
Tel: 0181 546 3368

Association of British Picture Restorers
Station Avenue, Kew, Surrey TW9 3QA
Tel: 0181 948 5644

Association of Illustrators
29 Bedford Square, London WC1B 3EG
Tel: 0171 636 4100

Association of Photographers
9 – 10 Domingo Street, London EC1Y 0TA
Tel: 0171 608 1441

British Actors' Equity Association (EQUITY)
8 Harley Street, London W1N 2AB
Tel: 0171 379 6000

British Association of Beauty Therapy and Cosmetology (BABTAC)
Suite 5, Wolseley House, Oriel Road, Cheltenham GL50 1TH
Tel: 01242 570 284

Broadcasting, Entertainment, Cinematograph Technicians Union (BECTU)
111 Wardour Street, London W1V 4AY
Tel: 0171 437 8506

Chartered Institute of Marketing
Moor Hall, Cookham, Maidenhead, Berks SL6 9QH
Tel: 01628 524 922

Chartered Society of Designers
29 Bedford Square, London WC1B 3EG
Tel: 0171 631 1510

CCN
Commercial Sales Office, Talbot House, Talbot St,
Nottingham NG1 5HF
Tel: 01159 410 888
Enquiries about credit status.

Enterprise Publications (Cambridge) Ltd
5 Station Road, Longstanton, Cambridge CB4 5DS
Tel: 01954 261 040
For booklets on starting and running your own business.

Institute of Public Relations
15 Northburgh Street, London EC1V 0PR
Tel: 0171 253 5151

Institute of Translators and Interpreters
377 City Road, London EC1V 1NA
Tel: 0171 713 7600

Market Research Society
15 Northburgh Street, London EC1V 0PR
Tel: 0171 490 4911

Musicians Union – National Office
60 – 62 Clapham Road, London SW9 0JJ
Tel: 0171 582 5566

National Association of Teleworkers
Weston, Honiton, Devon EX14 0PG
Tel: 01404 47467
Have members from all professions, both freelancers and employees, working at home.

National Union of Journalists (NUJ)
Acorn House, 314 Grays Inn Road, London
WC1X 8DP
Tel: 0171 278 7916
Members include cartoonists, crossword compilers, DTP workers, editors and sub-editors, feature writers, illustrators, journalists, newsreaders, photographers, public relations, reporters, script writers and translators.

Society of Authors
84 Drayton Gardens, London SW10 9SB
Tel: 0171 373 6642

Society of Freelance Editors and Proofreaders (SFEP)
The Administrator, 38 Rochester Road, London
NW1 9JJ
Tel: 0171 813 3113

Society of Indexers
38 Rochester Road, London NW1 9JJ
Tel: 0171 916 7809

Society of Picture Researchers and Editors (SPREd)
BM Box 259
London WC1N 3XX

Women in Publishing
c/o 12 Dyott Street, London WC1A 1DF

PERFECT BUSINESS WRITING

Peter Bartram

In every job, writing plays a part – and the ability to write well helps you to perform your job better. Good writing is important both for you and for your organization. It enables you to communicate effectively with your colleagues. It advances your career prospects. It contributes to the success of your company by improving communication with customers and suppliers – and it enhances the corporate image.

If you, like so many people, lack confidence in your writing ability, this book is the perfect answer.

£5.99 Net in UK only.

ISBN 0–7126–5534–4

THE PERFECT BUSINESS PLAN

Ron Johnson

A really professional business plan is crucial to success. This book provides a planning framework and shows you how to complete it for your own business in 100 easy to follow stages.

Business planning will help you to make better decisions today, taking into account as many of the relevant factors as possible. A carefully prepared business plan is essential to the people who will put money into the business, to those who will lend it money, and above all to the people who carry out its day to day management.

£5.99 Net in UK only.

ISBN 0–7126–5524–7

THE PERFECT PRESENTATION

Andrew Leigh and Michael Maynard

When everything seems to go right, you perform at your absolute best, your audience reacts enthusiastically and comes away inspired, then you've given the perfect presentation!

But success is underpinned by hard work, and the authors of this book provide the necessary framework on which to base your presentations, under the headings of the 'Five Ps': Preparation, Purpose, Presence, Passion and Personality.

Many major organizations have used material from the courses on which this book is based. Now you can gain those benefits – at a fraction of the cost.

£5.99 Net in UK only.

ISBN 0–7126–5536–0

THE PERFECT CV

Max Eggert

First impressions are vital – and your CV will be the first impression of you for most potential employers.

Whether you are applying for your first job or planning that all important career move, your CV will be the most potent strike weapon in your armoury. This concise and invaluable guide provides the blueprint for the perfect CV, which presents you and your skills and experience in the best possible way, and avoids the many easily made mistakes which swiftly antagonize prospective employers.

£5.99 Net in UK only.

ISBN 0–7126–5546–8